The White Witch's Book of Healing

The White Witch's Book of Healing

Weaving Magickal Rituals throughout
your Craft for Sacred Healing and
Reclamation of the Wild Witch Within

tgh.

LONDON

The White Witch's Book of Healing: Weaving Magickal Rituals throughout your Craft for Sacred Healing and Reclamation of the Wild Witch Within

The book information is catalogued as follows;
Author Name(s): Carly Rose
Title: The White Witch's Book of Healing: Weaving Magickal Rituals throughout your Craft for Sacred Healing and Reclamation of the Wild Witch Within
Description; First Edition

1st Edition, 2021

Book Design by Leah Kent
Cover Illustration by Hannah Nickolls

ISBN 978-1-914447-26-6 (paperback)
ISBN 978-1-914447-27-3 (ebook)

Prepared by That Guy's House Ltd.

www.ThatGuysHouse.com

edication

First and foremost, to my sun, moon and stars Amelie.

I cannot find strong enough words to
express how much I love you.

David and Leonie, my beautiful parents for
your sheer patience, belief, support and love

Kindness and patience
I can never thank you enough
for all you have done for me.

My little brother Allen for supporting me with my
work and inspiring me to do what I love.

The wild women that have stood by me in the light and
dark days - my soul family – Hannah, Kelly, Alex,
Mary, Rachael, Jade and Kellie.

All the amazing witches who listen to my podcast
and support my work – I am so honoured
and grateful for all of you!

Lastly to the ones that broke my heart – thank you for
fuelling the fire of transformation for this witch!!!!

Contents

Acknowledgments

Where do I start? Emma Mumford, the ultimate spiritual queen, thank you for showing up in my life and being such a blessing. I can never express how grateful I am for your patience when I was still growing as an author and a person writing this book. I will never forget the heart to heart we had regarding twin flames.

My long-lost Italian friend Jackie who gifted me the magnificent book 'Women who run with the Wolves' and a set of Ryder Waite tarot cards on my 21st birthday, and set me off on my witchy path as an adult.

Literary geniuses whose work inspires me on the daily – Clarissa Pinkola-Estes, Danielle Dulsky and musical genius Ben Howard whose words saw me through the darkest of days and the writing of this book.

Introduction

I class myself as a green and sea witch. I live in a Victorian flat with my beautiful daughter Amelie, Bowie our French bulldog and Tarot our tiny black cat. We have a home full of second hand French style furniture I have rescued and painted white, a small courtyard garden packed full of herbs and plants and the sea is at the end of our road. I have a healthy addiction to books, plants, tattoos, candles and of course witchcraft.

Witchcraft has always felt like coming home, it has gifted me a sense of belonging through working with nature and my deities, distracted my monkey mind in the early stages of addiction recovery with creating spells, getting out into nature to find items for my altar, logging my dreams in my dream book, using my money for books, candles and crystals instead of bottles of prosecco and enabled me to meet my witchy sisters within the witchcraft community.

Witchcraft had me stepping out of my comfort zone releasing a podcast purely on a whim only to have thousands of people subsequently listen to the show, many listeners contact me to say they too have struggled with issues of healing be it from drug or alcohol addiction, trauma, breakups, codependency or low self-worth. I was often asked for books I could recommend that would help them but I too had struggled to find books within the craft that could weave everything together that I felt I needed when I embarked on my healing journey.

I could never have envisaged this book would come to life, I also didn't imagine I would have a podcast that people around the world would listen to.

I felt pretty lost for most of my younger days, highly sensitive, I often transmuted my confused overwhelming emotions into anger that led to depression. I didn't know where my place in the world was and this led to a frustrating number of years where I put myself into the worst situations ever, shoplifting to orders whilst at secondary school, smoking marijuana we would steal from my friends dad on the walk to school, starting on cocaine at fifteen and a crack cocaine addiction by the age of twenty-one.

I viewed myself as a bad person at that time so I opted to stick with the people aboard that same boat. I knew there was a good person in me somewhere but she felt too inadequate and lowly around the bright light people doing positive things. She also felt overwhelmed with how much work she would have to do to heal so she wouldn't even attempt to get started.

My parents went through absolute hell with me but they never gave up. When I was on the brink of trying to buy heroin it was my dad I called to come clean and ultimately get clean. They never turned me away no matter how dark things got.

At the age of thirty five following many on and off attempts to seek mental health support with limited success I was diagnosed with emotional intensity disorder. This is a condition where you have heightened emotional sensitivity and intense reactions, it can affect your relationships, work, physical health and self- esteem and it is common for people with EID to look for coping mechanisms such as self-harm, substance abuse, impulsively spending money, binge eating, engaging in risky sex which all of course add to further problems.

These risky behaviors can help you feel better in the moment but cause no end of chaos and hurt to you and those around you in the long term. People with EID tend to experience unstable emotions and moods at such intensity along with chronic feelings of emptiness. I discovered that it can be common for EID suffererers to contemplate or even attempt suicide, around eighty percent of those with EID attempt suicide and deaths from suicide range between eight to ten percent.

Having this condition confirmed was life changing for me, I could finally start to understand my behaviour across my lifetime. The best support I received in the form of mental health came from counselling sessions with Sue, the first time I persisted with counselling and we have had sessions on and off for the last five years. I can never express how grateful I am to Sue, that one hour every fortnight was crucial and transformational. This book consists of all the work I did in between those sessions that intertwined with my craft.

On my mental health team I also had Lynda, my wonderful herbalist and true witch in every sense. In my darkest days I would attend consultations with her, sitting sobbing at the table in her apothecary that was adorned with a multitude of glass bottles of potions containing every herb you can possibly imagine lined up behind me on the wall. I was sceptical at first about what a herbalist could do to heal but my reasoning then was if marijuana and cocaine could create such effects then who was I to belittle herbal medicine?.

I explained to Lynda through floods of tears how broken I felt whilst she concocted a medicine that included wood betony, liquorice and lavender amongst other ingredients that seriously levelled me out. She will never know how grateful I was for those sessions in my early healing and how she got me on track.

After years of never being able to successfully take antidepressants or any tablets prescribed for mental health due to feeling progressively worse I had finally found a natural means of boosting my mood, giving me a foundation to start the work on my mind. None of this was a rosy period, we are talking a real dark night of the soul combined with the responsibility of being a single parent to my daughter, a full time career as a recruiter with some big targets, financial issues and a serious alcohol dependency.

For the majority of my life I just wanted my emotions to actually work for me, not against me. I turned to numbing out in a bid to not experience these feelings as I believe many of us do. Sitting in AA meeting rooms on and off for a couple of years I realised that most addicts and people with seriously intense healing to do often have such amazing and wild minds, many I have met are serious creatives but struggling with the emotional intensity of life.

In a nutshell I know what it's like to heal from addiction, low self-worth, suicidal thoughts and the belief you have nothing to offer this world. I have laid on the floor in the fetal position sobbing like an injured animal praying for everything to finish or cried guttural cries in the bathtub thinking life held nothing.

But I have also felt high on life being out in a golden corn field with my daughter at the height of summer. I have cried reading the most beautiful of books that spoke to my soul and also sitting at peace with myself in daily meditation and conversation with my deities. I have also felt pretty bloody amazing eating chips on the seafront with my best friend. The point is I have experienced the very depths of the darkness and realise that without those you cannot experience the highest of highs.

This book is for you my love, the one who feels that they will never ever be able to heal that particular hurt be it cast on you through addiction, trauma, toxic relationships or a lack of love for your beautiful soul. I know alone this book will not heal all your wounds however I hope it will provide comfort and solace and a way to weave your healing process into your craft.

This is an account of my own practices tackling my own drug and alcohol addiction, toxic relationships, codependency, suicidal thoughts and mental health issues. I am also aware my journey will always be ongoing and in no way straightforward or linear.

I recommend you start honouring your healing process by treating yourself to a beautiful notebook that you can use as a journal or book of shadows to document many of the rituals and your own personal findings as you work through this book.

I ask that whilst working through this book above all you treat yourself with the kindness and patience you so deserve and know I am sending you all the witchy love I can as we embark on this journey.

'Rough places show you what you're made of, child........ Rough places ask you who you wish to become, stripped raw and bare. Rough places force you to come to grips with what you truly want in your most trying moments. Do you believe me?'

Danielle Dulsky - Seasons of Moon and Flame

The Worst Witch

You might have come across this book as a result of listening to my podcast. I am the host of The White Witch Podcast which first aired at Samhain 2019 and this is when the real magick began in my life.

I hope that by reading this book you can bring out the magick in your life too! My intention with the pages within this book is to conjure up and bring inspiration and healing to your craft. I have elaborated on some of the content I covered on my podcast but also thrown into the cauldron many additional practices that have helped me on my own crooked path.

Without sounding too dramatic, but failing miserably, witchcraft changed my life beyond comparison. I started out as that little girl who never desired to be a princess, I only ever wanted to be a witch. That was the dream!

Watching the Worst Witch film that starred Tim Curry and Fairuza Balk back in the eighties had me fantasising about attending witch school long before Harry Potter came on the scene. Combine that with being packed off for long hot summers staying in

Bodmin, Cornwall where my grandparents lived, they would tell us the historical lore of the local witch trees, stone circles, druids, folk magick and took us on trips to the Boscastle Witch Museum, all of these experiences strengthened my curiosity and thirst for the craft.

As a teen in the nineties I was obsessed with witchy themed films such as Hocus Pocus, The Craft and Practical Magic. I always had an affinity for the mystical, anything witchy would sing to my soul and have me feeling aligned. The fixation continued yet in late teen years rapidly began to be replaced with a penchant for cheap alcohol, clubbing and badly behaved boys.

My childhood was pretty idyllic but as soon as puberty hit I was desperately insecure and unhappy within myself, a destructive angry whirlwind trying to seek some form of happiness mainly through hedonism. Witchcraft was abandoned temporarily aside from me picking up the odd Silver RavenWolf book now and again or re-watching one of my favourite witchy films.

During my early twenties I demonstrated hugely self sabotaging destructive behaviour, my first serious relationship was with an alcoholic. I didn't realise my boyfriend was addicted to alcohol until we moved in together, his addiction began as a result of being left for dead for a number of hours in an alley following a hit and run accident. His addiction increased till he eventually upped the ante and added crack cocaine to his battalion of vices. I was so naive at this point I didn't even know what crack cocaine was, had never even heard of it let alone comprehended how addictive it was. I succumbed to trying it one day after having a few drinks, my boyfriend resisted allowing me to try it at first, fast forward three weeks and I was addicted, desperate for my next hit. Crack had me in its claw-like grip.

I was a high functioning addict in that I could get up on time for work (sometimes I hadn't even slept following a session taking crack cocaine), take a shower, put on my makeup and jump on the train to London to be at work for half eight. I had to keep my job to finance my drug habit yet at this point I hadn't grasped how much this demon-like drug had taken over my life. I remember my best friend from school Francesca finding out about me using, she kindly attempted to intervene with her best intentions, dragging me along to a counselling session for addiction. On another occasion she turned up at my house for an evening out we had arranged, I asked my boyfriend to pretend I was out whilst I hid upstairs high as a kite, so high I couldn't even face her but selfishly I wanted to carry on with the crack cocaine session I had already started.

The next day I woke up with soul destroying feelings of guilt combined with a comedown and sent her a huge bouquet of flowers to apologise, gradually and understandably I lost that friendship along with any feelings of respect from my faithful friend and deservedly so.

Life went on for a while like this, just working and taking drugs. There were nights me and my partner would get high and end up having a punch up, I remember smashing his head against a bannister repeatedly in defence for him attacking me first, I recall feeling so disgusted thinking this is so messed up, I love this person and we are killing each other. Another time he had to drag me to A and E following me slashing my wrists, I was full of a cocktail of drugs and alcohol and had no idea what I was doing or why. I remember walking through A and E with blood all over me, bandages on my wrist as I met the look of disgust at the state I was in from a woman within the hospital waiting room.

Me and my boyfriend reached a point where we no longer felt enough of a hit from crack, it began to feel like decaf. We had started to increase our usage for a better high and then we began to discuss trying to score heroin.

I honestly believe something, someone or perhaps just my intuition knew that if we reached that point one of us would die. I truly believe this is what led me to call my dad from a payphone at my local train station in London at five in the morning following an intense drug session. I realised I couldn't do this anymore and would rather break my parents heart by explaining I was an addict then keep travelling down this road and have them identify my body at the morgue. I wanted to get clean.

I moved from the concrete jungle of south London to my parents' new home they had recently moved to in the depths of the countryside in East Sussex, no dealers anywhere that I knew and could get to, It was a mile walk to civilisation. My parents confiscated my bank cards and took the total reign of my life in a bid to help get me clean. I kept my job in London but on a few occasions I would go off track and go missing following on from work if I managed to get money out of the bank via forms of ID I had or through borrowing money from friends. I would run back to visit my old boyfriend, not to see him so much but so we could take crack cocaine together.

This went on for a little while until it started to dawn on me, I was beginning to like my new life without the drugs and the boyfriend. I really wanted to knock it on the head once and for all, this was further solidified following someone we knew who died within his early thirties as a result of using crack cocaine.

I stopped using crack but some of this was helped by upping my alcohol intake, in effect I swapped out one addiction for another. I didn't drink everyday, however I embarked on binge sessions with the goal of reaching the blackout unconscious stage, it was all or nothing from the first drink to black out.

I yearned to feel nothing, I was overwhelmingly sensitive to everything, peoples comments and behaviours, my own issues around my appearance and who I was overall, just never feeling enough. Alcohol and drugs helped in the moment with anxiety and provided false confidence when I needed it most. Alcohol and drugs are of course both depressants so the side effects I experienced often were increased anxiety and depression following a binge drinking session yet I couldn't correlate the two, therefore the cycle continued. I couldn't fathom a time where I would no longer rely entirely on some sort of vice.

A marker on my life that heralded a small return to myself and the craft came when I met Jackie through my work within a private healthcare company, insanely spiritual and witchy and a fellow Leo, she gifted me my first set of Tarot cards and a copy of one of my favourite books 'Women who Run with the Wolves' by Clarissa Pinkola Estes for my 21st birthday.

Meeting Jackie and the influences she brought to my life I felt a flicker of light and hope within me, an understanding of who I was or could be. Jackie and I worked in a large company but I genuinely think we were drawn to each other like magnets from the get go as kindred spirits. She is a wild haired beautiful older woman who at the time was in her sixties but looked in her mid-forties without having had any work done. I believe she could see I was in desperate need of her spiritual guidance or she could sense I would be receptive to it. She talked to me at length about angels, tarot cards and spirits. I was intrigued and couldn't get enough of what she would begin to teach me.

One day Jackie relayed the tale of her husband's demise, he had worked as an Italian diver and one day she was holding her young son on the beach on the italian coast waiting for him to surface from the seas depths and come back to the shore following a dive. He never surfaced and a search party never found his body. Despite such a traumatic loss my dear friend couldn't have had a bigger heart and love and lust for life. She was the embodiment of how I would love to feel in my own skin. She may never read this, but I wish she could know how she truly changed the course of my life and how thankful I am to her.

Following meeting Jackie I worked with my tarot cards regularly, I frequented psychics and bought spiritual and witchy books and resources, sowing the seeds for what I would return to in full force later on down the line.

I kept collecting the witchy books, dipping in and out of them, every now and again I would carry out a ritual yet I wasn't fully committed to identifying and initiating myself as a witch.

Up till now my romantic relationship history was chequered at best, generally dating alpha males with narcissistic traits. I am by no means an angel but the combination of an empath who is outwardly confident but hugely co-dependent was a great match for a narcissist. Enter stage left the boyfriend that nearly did finish me off.

They say there is a fine line between love and hate, I never truly understood that sentiment until our relationship. We met and it was literal fireworks both physically, and mentally. We were a really powerful couple combined, when we were good we were very very good but when we were bad we were horrid.

Cue five years of toxicity and codependency, when we broke up for the hundredth time I moved to a new home with my daughter without him. This had occurred before but instead of him chasing me again in our toxic cat and mouse relationship he met another woman online within about two weeks of us separating.

I hadn't prepared myself for the grieving process or untangling my codependency, I struggled to cope with how quickly he had moved on and had shacked up with someone else. I started to drink around two to three bottles of prosecco or merlot a night around three to four times a week. It depended on how hungover I was from the night before, I must have cried for months.

My ex taunted me with his new partner, I obsessed over them, sickenly I allowed him to cheat on her with me at my lowest point. I didn't truly want to be with him to be honest, in hindsight I was trauma bonded to him. I had zero self-respect for myself and began to feel sorry for his new girlfriend because of what we had done. I didn't really care what happened to me at this point. I was on my knees with feelings of hopelessness, guilt for the new girlfriend and disgust at my alcoholism, lack of self-worth and allowing myself to behave in that way. I was still high functioning taking care of my responsibilities but the cracks were huge, I just plastered over them with alcohol or by setting huge unrealistic goals for my life thinking they might inspire me enough to get out of the hole I had hurled myself into.

This period of my life went on for much longer than it should have, one day I was lying on the floor of my hallway completely hungover, ugly crying until I reached a decision to try to end my life (again) by trying to cut my wrists. I pulled myself up off the floor and began to take knives from the kitchen drawers in preparation. Honestly something kicked in then that I couldn't go on like this and I couldn't do this to my daughter..

Things had to change and change they did following that day. None of this happened quickly, there was still a lot of pain to go through to get there. I started recognising how awful alcohol made me feel mentally yet it took me a good two years before I finally started going to AA meetings and addressing my binge drinking properly.

I attended counselling sessions throughout this period, my counsellor Sue is still with me to this day and has seen the change but it's been close to five years for things to come good. Far from a clinical counsellor she straddles the line between spirituality and psychotherapy which worked perfectly for me, it was this combination that helped me move forward.

Spiritually nothing changed for a while, I would read spirituality books all the time in a period where Gabrielle Bernstein, Danielle Laporte and the like were most popular, I also inhaled spirituality and witchcraft podcasts and YouTube videos.

I started to have this insistent voice in my head asking me to read my witchcraft books, it didn't make any sense to me as to why but I eventually succumbed.

Through this period of intensively studying my craft through my books and multiple resources I began to resound and align again with my craft. I recognised how like life, nature has dark and light, good and bad and the need for masculine and feminine energy. I had always wanted to be a witch as a child and here I was in my thirties finally identifying with the title, I think my ancestors, deities and angels must have straight out face palmed themselves thinking finally she has got the message!

For months all I did was inhale the vast collection of witch books I had been collecting over the course of my life, I bought or borrowed every witch book I could lay my hands on. Gradually I began to feel so passionate and inspired, it was like a switch went on inside of me and I began to come back to life. This new sensation encouraged me to get out in my garden where I discovered I was a true green witch through growing my own herbs, tomatoes, squashes, courgettes, flowers, lilies, anything I could - I discovered a true magick in nature. Stepping out into my garden barefoot in the spring and summer to look at the progress of my babies, watering and caring for them in my tiny garden is true bliss.

I then discovered another love through witchcraft for making things from my produce. I used my grown vegetables and herbs in some kitchen witchery. I made smoke cleansing wraps using my own herbs and cut my own flowers to use for decoration. I learnt how to make my own candles from scratch, I felt like a true witch standing over a huge saucepan which was akin to having a vast cauldron, heating up the wax before hand pouring the wax into glass candle jars as I listened to music by Peter Gundry and Ben Howard. I cast intentions over the candles and added crystals to them and they became more beautiful and sacred to me than any candles I could buy at the shops. These tasks seem so simple but these moments brought me out of a very dark place.

I began to love my own company, it gave me time to focus on my craft, I started to like myself and understand who I was and what I was passionate about. I found solace in working with goddesses such as

Hekate and the Morrigan – through these deities I began to understand that strong women can be destructive and not have a shiny wholesome history yet still do good things. I finally learnt that the more I drank alcohol the less I felt connected to my craft so slowly but surely I began to clean up my drinking and began to eat better, this helped my connection to nature and life overall.

I began to accept myself as sensitive and honour my feelings and intuition, I realised that I could pick up and be affected by an individual's energy or the energy in a room, I used reading people's body language as a positive and I started to pay close attention to the prophetic dreams or messages I experienced.

Like the time I dreamt of hugging my ex-boyfriend, crying and saying goodbye to him as he told me he was moving to the west country. That dream stayed on my mind all day until I caved, breaking the no contact rule I had set for myself messaging him to ask if he was relocating anytime soon. He quickly responded in shock, he revealed he had just signed a contract a couple of dates before for a job in Somerset but hadn't told anyone about it. I think he was a bit scared of me and my prophecy following that!.

At this point I was Switzerland when it came to my ex, completely neutral, and honestly just unsure how we had ever got together, but looking back now I am so grateful for him breaking my heart because it was the catalyst I needed for me to completely unravel and then begin to heal. I could finally let him go and wish him and his new girlfriend all the best but actually mean it - that was truly empowering.

After reading endless witchcraft books and working on my craft for a good while I got the idea in my head to begin a podcast to help me market a little witchy company I was planning on starting up. The idea was that I would make spell candles, witchy hoodies, T-shirts and prints. Just a side hustle alongside my day job to allow me to enjoy creating, once I got started with the podcast out of nowhere it began to take off really quickly, I got to number one in the UK spirituality chart and various countries across the world.

Instead of making candles or anything else I had originally planned on selling I just focused on creating the podcast. I loved the process of researching and building my knowledge for each episode. It also gave me an excuse to buy more witchcraft books as I kicked off each show with a book review. My brother Allen had previously worked as a Sound Engineer for Abbey Road Records and he offered to master the podcast for me in his own studio within the basement of his house to make it sound more professional.

I had no idea what I was doing with the podcast, I had bought a microphone so just got on with talking about my witchy research that I spent time putting together, I was in my element. About five months in I discovered that there were podcast charts – I hadn't even realised. What's hilarious is that my podcast had charted at number one on the Apple Spirituality chart in the UK and some other countries, yet I had been blissfully unaware just recording new episodes and oblivious to whether or not anyone was listening. I was happy in the flow of creating.

Although this first chapter is about my story, it's retold as a means to demonstrate how powerful the craft really is, to explain how it has changed my life beyond comparison and to demonstrate how it can do the same for you. Ultimately this is a collection of some of my favourite parts of the craft that I feel can be so valuable for your own healing journey.

Let witchcraft show us the light and dark in all, the necessity for the various Mother, Maiden, Crone stages of life and find comfort that through destruction and chaos comes new beginnings.

Witchcraft offers us a lifetime of learning and as long as you put in your best intentions and harm none do as ye will.

The Dark Night of the Soul

I feared writing this chapter the most, it has haunted me from the moment I decided this is how the book needed to begin.

If you are experiencing your own dark night of the soul you will likely view it as a curse that has taken you to the very depths of hell, an experience you fear you may never escape from. If you have survived a dark night of the soul you will likely see this as a blessing that changed your life completely.

The dark night of the soul experience can be triggered following a major event in your life such as a near death experience, a terminal illness, the loss of someone you love, a separation or divorce or even losing faith in your religion, overall some form of major event that shakes up your life.

My own dark night of the soul followed on from my separation with my fiance who I mentioned in the last chapter. Leading up to the separation I had a consistent voice in my head, similar to that same voice I recounted to you that told me to read my witchcraft books. I like to call that my wild woman voice, she started off every now and then gently asking me 'when are you going to leave him Carly?' at that stage I would just shrug her off and retort 'but why would I?'

On face value I had everything I needed, the huge new house, money, success in my career, nice cars, designer handbag, weekends of going to fancy restaurants necking champagne. Everything was available to me, I had the showroom house that I tidied and cleaned and invited people over to show off in, serve up fancy food and drinks whilst my 6 foot 6 charming partner played the host.

That voice was insistent and the longer I continued to brush her off the more that wild woman started looking for other outlets to call me home. She was attracted to music and books that spoke of nature and the wild, she started me off listening to podcasts, providing me with little sparks of inspiration regarding other more rewarding fulfilling work and hobbies I could be doing, she began to make me aware of how much alcohol I consumed just to make an evening with my fiancé bearable, she put fleeting intuitive thoughts into my head regarding my so called friends and fiancé uncovering who they really were. That wild woman's voice from inside started getting louder and more insistent until I heard her practically every five minutes, almost like contractions signifying a new birth. Urgently repeating the same statement 'when are you going to leave him Carly'. I wasn't laughing it off anymore, I knew she could see everything I had decided to bury.

That wild woman started to seep into my being, I began to question things and I began to get awkward.

I started to examine the relationships I had with my friends and fiancé, did they have my best interests at heart? What did we really have in common at the end of the day? Did this big house with its empty rooms and many things make me happy? Why was I beginning to feel repulsed at how much money I spent every single weekend on bored alcohol fuelled dinners with my fiancé, nights that deadened my wild spirit and enabled me to be drunk enough not to want to start an argument with him when he was particularly obnoxious.

Then the wild woman started to roar and she had had enough. I finished the engagement, I handed back the ring, I found a beautiful home of my own for me and my daughter and my familiars, I made the arrangements and I destroyed every piece of that Stepford Wives existence burning it down to the ground. If I could have danced around the flames I would.

The first few weeks were great, I was free, the wild woman had her way. She was appeased, three weeks of house warming parties ensued, celebrating with some of the remaining toxic friends I was yet to finish things with. I had the wild women within me now, akin to some Celtic goddess forging the way ahead and life felt good. That was until I couldn't hear her anymore, that bold confidence I had departed and I realised she had likely left to rescue some other fair maiden who needed to have her blinkers removed. This is when my dark night of the soul really began and brought me to my knees. I consider my dark night as the death of the old me. I often wonder how I survived this period of my life because the darkness almost consumed me.

Not due to the breakup, nor the terrible friends or the alcohol dependency. This was a complete annihilation of everything that I believed in and who I thought I was.

The dark night of the soul is holistic - a spiritual, mental and physical experience. Physically you may feel exhausted regardless of how much you sleep, you might feel deathly or hollow inside. like the walking dead with an aching heart to the point of physical pain.

Mentally you may feel suicidally depressed, anxious, full of despair, lonely, hopeless and as though you cannot see a way out of the darkness. Spiritually it can have you questioning why the universe, god, goddess, your deities, ancestors, whomever you work with or believe in could or would ever put you through this pain and suffering, feeling as though they have forgotten or betrayed you and as a result have you questioning your faith or spirituality.

You may find yourself asking if this is your karma or what you might have done to be plagued with this complete existential crisis. The dark night can also affect your relationships, you may find you struggle with connection with friends or family as they are unable to comprehend what you are going through.

The dark night of the soul is a complete deconstruction of the ego and our belief systems, it's a death for all former meaning within our life but this death gives us the opportunity to be reborn. Working fully through the dark night experience can provide us with a complete transformation into who we are truly meant to be.

The term Dark Night of the Soul stemmed from the 1600's poem ' Dark Night of the Soul' or 'La noche oscura del alma' penned by Spanish monk Saint John of the Cross where he outlined his own dark night experience. Saint John struggled in writing the poem to convey that the dark night is far from an experience of depression which today can be treated somewhat effectively through counselling, medication, changes in thought patterns, lifestyle and other experiences/methods.

You cannot bargain your way out of the dark night of the soul experience through the use of these methods either, the experience calls on you to work through this on your own without the use of any map. Everyone's experience and reason for arriving at this awakening is completely different, meaning no one can provide any specific guidance to your unique dark night.

Our mind is rational so it struggles to work through the dark night experience, seeking out solutions to put things right when in essence we can only navigate the process by surrendering to the despair and desolation we are in the midst of.

Our mind will confuse matters by offering up cures for our happiness, our energy levels will naturally be low both physically and mentally due to the internal battle we are constantly facing, despite this our mind will lead us on a merry dance, encouraging us to take up new interests or work to new goals, perhaps influenced by former ways we have sought out and achieved happiness.

This can feel like a form of torment, going round in circles, treading different paths in a bid to score happiness. Our brain is simply trying to work in our favour through stepping around the pain, confusion and anguish that the dark night brings us.

The only way to work through this journey successfully is to start by surrendering to the knowledge that happiness cannot come from relationships, money or material objects and that happiness just is. We can become stuck in a loop of chasing happiness without accepting that we can feel it in the present without having to do anything. A somewhat frustrating notion but at the same time should help you realise that there is nothing you can buy, do or bring into your life that will change your current circumstances, all that is asked of you is that you allow these feelings and questions wash over you without trying to chase them out.

You cannot pray, bargain or barter your way out of the dark night of the soul, nor can you covet and collect material objects or use relationships as a band aid. The solution is to fully surrender to and experience the transformational process.

You may still find yourself embarking on different paths in a bid to remove the curse of the dark night of the soul. You may even come to a time where you believe you have broken the curse. This is referred to as the halo effect, the illusion that you have finally made your way out of your dark night experience where we might start to feel better, as though we have finally found a route that has taken us from that pit of despair only to find this comes crashing down and we find ourselves back where we started from or cast even further into the darkness.

'There is no coming to consciousness without pain. People will do anything, no matter how absurd, to avoid facing their own soul. One does not become enlightened by imagining figures of light, but by making the darkness conscious'

Carl Gustav Jung

My own dark night of the soul experience looked like this, excessive dependency on alcohol and drinking alone, constant exhaustion, attempts to talk or rekindle the relationship with my ex-partner to obtain the former happiness we had in the beginning of our relationship, risky sexual relationships seeking sexual highs, seeking attention and validation from the opposite sex, overspending through buying items I thought would improve my status, comfort eating, always being in the company of others (mainly toxic friendships) so as not to be alone and to provide distraction and low level comfort rather than having to deal with my thoughts.

You may find within your own dark night of the soul that every aspect of your life feels flawed, despite how much focus you place within specific areas things still seem to fall apart and solidify the feeling of being betrayed, forgotten or as though this might be some form of karma.

Relationships can really be tricky during the dark night experience as we can feel as though no one understands what we are going through. Even if people we know report going through the same, their experience will be their own so they cannot provide much guidance to work through your own personal unique journey.

Speaking to friends and family can be tricky in that it may trigger their own fears, insecurities and even dark night experiences if they have had one. For me, confiding in trusted friends and family made the process even more difficult, from the outside people thought I was just depressed over a long expected breakup when truth be told I was having a complete existential crisis for which the breakup was a mere singular puzzle piece. Instead of relying on friends and family so much, I worked on self-soothing which originally came in the form of drinking and crying but progressed to a healthier form through baths, books, counselling, journaling through to shadow work.

I began a relationship during this period of my life that did help me in some respects with my self-worth and understanding my mental health better. My new partner also encouraged and took me along to my first ever AA meeting. Our relationship stopped me from seeking out risky sexual experiences and I felt some form of comfort. I still felt alone within this relationship as I was still on my journey through the dark night. That was until the wild woman made her return.

You may recall me opening the book claiming that witchcraft saved me. I was three years on from my dark night experience by now and her message this time round started off a humble little suggestion of 'read your witchcraft books'.

If ever you have heard that little voice within you will know how much it makes you question your sanity but this time round even more so, what had my witchcraft books got to do with anything?. At least last time the message she had was relevant! I ignored the message at first, still not convinced I had got it right or if it really was her making a return.

But then she got louder and I knew it was unmistakably her, I found myself immersing myself into nature through gardening and being by the sea, I started making candles with crystals in and cast them with intentions for joy and abundance, I began making sage wraps using my own herbs, wrapping them with pretty twine and adding crystals and all the while, of course pouring over my witchcraft books. I was compelled and for months I reread my books, I frequented my local library and ordered anything related to the craft I could get my hands on and spent all my money that was once allocated to prosecco and vodka on witchcraft books. I planned on selling my candles, homemade soaps and sage bundles at farmers markets and online, once I had made that decision a path began to unfold for me with opportunities and encouragement dropping in my lap abundantly.

Once deciding I was going to take this path I decided to get a crescent moon tattoo on my wedding ring finger to symbolise being married to this new path and lifestyle. My partner was so angry I had this tattoo done and our relationship ended that day following an argument about said tattoo although the breakup had, in all honesty been in the post. At the time I assumed he was joking but little did I know the universe had other plans for us both.

Not long after that day my former partner discovered that he had a child he had never known about from a previous relationship over ten years ago, a couple months after his discovery he ended up shacking up with his childs mother and then getting married. I felt like the wild woman was within me again therefore I didn't need to shed a tear, after all I had married my craft and new endeavours. I believed I had left this relationship unscathed.

Months went past of me making the podcast, fully committed and thriving in my new healthier lifestyle, fully committed to the craft and my work. That was until my ex-partner reached out to me, reality hit and came crashing down making me realise I had simply been experiencing my own halo effect and still had more work to do to get through the process. I surrendered to grieving this relationship and the disappointment that I hadn't found my own happy ever after. At this point I was still attached to the idea that a relationship could bring me out of my dark night of the soul and bring me finite happiness.

I believe the circumstances that led to my dark night of the soul didn't fully break me, this karmic relationship provided the final nail in the coffin bringing me to my knees again to fully work through my spiritual awakening. I believe the wild woman knew what was unfolding or had heard conversations I wasn't privy to that involved my former partner and that's why her calls began to get louder at that specific time. I had to immerse myself back into the darkness again whilst also balancing working on the new life I had started to cultivate with the podcast and my creative work whilst my heart was broken, not only for my ex but all manner of reasons that I still couldn't fathom.

The dark night of the soul can leave us longing for something intangible, a form of comfort or sense of home that we have never had or known. I had a broken heart over multiple relationships with friends and lovers and an archive of festering and untouched wounds to untangle. This was the stage of the dark night of the soul that brought me to discover shadow work, a process that led me to the biggest leap within my healing journey, working successfully through wounds that went back to my childhood.

Shadow work whilst you are in your dark night of the soul is a vital purging process that takes the power away from your shadow and something we will deep dive into shortly. Although there isn't a map for how to work through your personal experience of the dark night of the soul, the following pointers should help you move through the process in its entirety.

Honouring the Dark Night of the Soul

Bury the Bones
Surrender to the grief, depression and pain. Don't fight the overwhelming emotions, instead of trying to step around them, go deep into and through them. Cry as much as you need to, scream, fully experience the death of the old you.

This too shall pass
When you are experiencing a dark night of the soul it can feel relentless, you can lose all hope and feel as though there is no light at the end of the tunnel. Remind yourself regularly that this too shall pass.

Shadow Work
Unravel all of your patterns, behaviours, beliefs and emotions in order to uncover your shadow and remove its power over you. The shadow work chapter will support and guide you through this process.

Divine Guidance
Seek out messages or signs from the universe, deities, angels, ancestors. Whomever you work with or believe in spiritually and accept however they may come to help guide you out of the darkness.

Resurrection

Begin to witness yourself fully return to life, you should start to see that the dark night of the soul was a blessing not a curse. Start to move forward with your life, you may find your goals, desires and mindset have completely transformed. The dark night of the soul precedes a complete spiritual awakening.

——— ◆◇◆ ———

If your dark night of the soul starts at the hands of another individual it is believed by some that before we are incarnated here on earth we sign a soul contract with specific individuals who will lead us to our dark night of the soul. These karmic relationships are said to be necessary for both souls to resolve within this lifetime.

During the dark night you may feel that you have been thrown to the wolves or left out in the cold but if you work with any spiritual beings, be they deities, angels or ancestors it is said that although they hate to witness our pain they are still there, but this is a necessary part of our evolution to grow.

Following on from the dark night of the soul you may find you have an increased empathy towards others and ability to see their pain or suffering, an overall appreciation for everything, a sense of calm and peace, the ability to experience more joy within your life, less want or need for external objects as you know they cannot complete you, you no longer require external validation, better clarity and understanding of what you do not need or enjoy within your life, better trust in your own intuition, seeing reality for what it really is, an acceptance of why events played out and why they happened to you, no longer viewing yourself as a victim within your story, a better trust within your spiritual, religious beliefs or the universe as a whole and an acceptance of events and emotions and thoughts that show up for you.

Although you experience a spiritual awakening following a dark night of the soul you can and will likely still feel pain through the events or experiences that have happened to you in the past. It won't bring you to a point where the slate is cleared from all of your past hurts nor provide you with immunity from the same going forward or a further dark night experience. Spiritual awakening following a dark night of the soul experience does provide permanence that can lead you to make better choices and decisions in more alignment with your soul that should see your life going forward an entirely different experience. My life before my dark night feels as if it never happened or like a bad dream which is a common feeling for many.

Looking back on my own dark night of the soul experience I can now look on it as one of the greatest and most necessary events within my life. Consider the many gods and goddesses who caused chaos throughout mythology doing as they pleased in a bid to seek their own inner peace whilst they fully embraced their own darkness and inner turmoil. I like to think us mere mortals work to the same principles emerging from our own dark night of the soul understanding our true self and our strength but also making peace with and accepting our darkness.

Deities

A deity refers to a god or goddess. One of the most invaluable parts of my practice has been researching, honouring and working with deities. It is said you can honour more than one, you may wish to honour a god and a goddess to utilise the blend of masculine and feminine energy, you may have different deities that you familiarise yourself with over the course of your practice and work with at different times of your life. You might decide that you are a pantheist, this means you believe the universe and deity are one and the same. You might decide to become a henotheist who believes there are multiple deities but only works with one.

You might find working with a deity isn't for you, many Wiccans and pagans tend to work with gods and goddesses, some witches do not class themselves as either yet still opt to work with a deity. This is simply my personal experience of how worshipping deities has helped me in my journey and within my craft.

You may find that specific gods or goddesses call out to you and you find yourself working with them, alternatively you may want to research individual deities and see which ones most align with you.

I highly recommend carrying out as much research as you can into each deity when you are deciding on who to work with, it's seen to be of the utmost respect in order to fully understand your chosen god or goddess.

It's key to research their history, traits and items that are symbolic of them, for example, identifying which items they like to have made as offerings. Many of the offerings we make to deities align with their legend. A basic example to give would be working with Persephone, you may want to offer up pomegranates or narcissus flowers. This link is made through when Persephone was given a pomegranate in the underworld by a small spirit boy from which she ate six seeds, she was blissfully unaware that her mother Demeter and her father Zeus were currently making a decree that if she ate nothing in the underworld she could return home. The narcissus flower relates to the flower Persephone picked whilst in the fields with her mother Demeter. As she picked this flower, its type she had never come across before, a hole erupted in the ground from which Hades emerged on a chariot, kidnapping Persephone dragging her to the underworld.

I found myself drawn to Hekate as my first deity to honour, I genuinely felt I could relate to her as she had a penchant for the underdog or misfits in society, an ability to fit in with people at differing levels and she was a lover of solitude. Notoriously fierce she also demonstrated being humble, Hekate was also unwilling to sacrifice her independent nature for marriage, something I repeatedly felt I had been bumping up against in my own romantic relationships! Once I found Hekate I had this knowing feeling she was the deity for me.

Hekate was also known for visiting cemeteries at night. I have often been teased by friends for being a taphophile, someone who loves to visit graveyards. Even as a kid, me and my brother had a graveyard at the back of our garden for our former pets that we would tend to. The goth in me was real!

Identifying Hekate as the deity I wanted to honour was just the beginning, my next hurdle was to see if Hekate would even want to work with me. I cannot stress how important it is to fully research your god or goddess before you even consider any approach, carrying out any ritual or initiation to work with them or asking for their assistance. Once I felt I had successfully exhausted all the information I could find on Hekate I then began making plans to carry out a ritual to make her acquaintance and figured out which offerings I should provide and how to call upon her.

Some deities may have specific ways you should approach them, for example it's said to be wise to bow down to the Morrigan as within lore pertaining to her this is the reverence she expected from Cu Chulainn, a mighty warrior whom she introduced herself to as a Great Queen whilst offering up her assistance to, yet other deities wouldn't expect the same level of approach.

To connect with any deity you can honour them through making offerings, prayers, meditating and acts of devotion. You may wish to add to your altar pictures depicting them and items that symbolise them specifically, perhaps even pieces of art, poetry or writing you might have created with them in mind or as your muse. Ensure that all approaches to your deity come from the heart, your energy must be pure and you should be fully present. If you offer a halfhearted approach expect a halfhearted response. Its key once you have consulted your deity to make sure you listen to what they have to say, be that through any synchronicities, dreams and the like. One of the main errors I am guilty of at times is to ask for their guidance but not always paying attention to the messages that are relayed to me.

You can work with your deity/deities in a number of ways, you may wish to play music or create a playlist of songs that you feel have association to them, talk to them about what's happening in your life, tell them what you love about them, explain the traits in them that you would like to develop or possess, leave them regular offerings, incorporate items on your altar that symbolise them, carry out activities that you feel honour them, for example for Hekate you could visit graveyards, for Aphrodite you may wish to visit the sea and offer up rose quartz to her in honour of romantic and self-love. I regularly call Hekate and the Morrigan to join me when I cast a circle and carry out any spell work and I express to them both what I am grateful for.

Once you have fully introduced yourself to your deity don't be afraid to pray to them and ask for assistance when you need it. During some of my darkest times I have called upon Hekate and the Morrigan to see if they might listen to what is troubling me and if they can help. Not every approach has to involve elaborate ritual and consistency is key to develop your relationship with your deity. Don't be afraid to have more than one god or goddess to work with but also don't feel guilty if you feel your time with one particular deity ends up being just for a season or specific period within your life, ensure you honour and thank them for all they have brought to your life and for the help they have provided. You may also find that some deities might not respond or work with you and it's best to keep searching until you have found the right deity for you.

From experience I know that once you finally develop a relationship with a deity you might be amazed at how powerful they are and their ability to turn things around for you in the most dramatic of ways you couldn't ever fathom. With this in mind I urge you to carefully consider that which you wish for and ensure you treat the sacred relationships with your deity/deities in the highest regard but overall enjoy this magickal connection!

Aphrodite

You may find certain deities make themselves known to you, I had a particular time of my life where I asked Hekate and the Morrigan to help me in the area of self love and relationships. Aphrodite made herself known to me very quickly thereafter, she had never been a goddess who appeared much on my radar, the deities I already worked with couldn't be more different. I spent a few weeks flirting with the idea of working with Aphrodite, she came through aesthetically to me first. I found myself flicking through images of the sea and mermaids, listening to songs relating to love and sex, my altar began to become very ethereal with pinks and whites and even angel wings.

I bought a handful of pink kunzite, angel aura quartz and rose angel aura quartz and began researching Aphrodite to produce a podcast episode on her. She really took hold of me, I was knee deep in my research on her and once the podcast episode had gone out I felt as though she had entered my life to teach me a few things, firstly regarding loving myself but also loving others. It's still possible to have your own toxic traits that you need to correct before coming to any relationship and this is something I needed to address.

Aphrodite is a wonderful deity to work with for self love, romantic relationships and also if you want to have a child or to find the right partner to start a family with.

Aphrodite is one of the twelve Greek Olympians, she represents beauty, love, procreation and sexuality. In Greek mythology she is said to have risen from the sea foam upon a scallop shell as a fully formed woman following the Greek sky god Uranus's genitals being thrown into the water. Her mother is said to be Greek Titaness Dionne.

Out of all the goddesses Aphrodite was said to be the most beautiful, all the gods and many mere mortals were struck by her beauty and ultimately fell in love with her. A multitude of fights broke out until Zeus decided to halt the arguments by marrying her off to the ugliest of all the gods - Hephaestus, god of metal-working and fire. Aphrodite was dissatisfied with the arrangement and went on to have many affairs whilst in the marriage with Aries the God of War, Hermes the Messenger God, Poseidon, God of the Sea and Adonis, a mortal.

Aphrodite was said to have no shame when it came to her sexual prowess and embraced it entirely, she had many children by many lovers and is known as a wonderful deity to work with for fertility or even finding the right partner to start a family with.

Aphrodite was the original mistress of seduction, she held power in the areas of love and sexual desire combined with the ability to make mortals fall instantly in love with one another or to reunite warring couples in a bid to enable them to enjoy love together once more.

Aphrodite was the beholder of a magic girdle that she would often share with her fellow goddesses, once she wore this magic girdle anyone she happened to encounter would fall in love with her.

Aphrodite earnt herself the title 'fairest of them all' amongst the goddesses following fellow goddess Eros tossing a golden apple with the words 'fairest of them all' inscribed upon it amongst the goddesses Hera, Athena and Aphrodite. An argument ensued between the goddesses as to who was most worthy of the apple and the coveted 'fairest of them all' title which Zeus took it upon himself to settle, calling on Paris, prince of Troy for his assistance. All three goddesses were quick to try to bribe Paris for the title, Hera offered him power over his enemies, Athena offered him infinite wisdom and Aphrodite...... the most beautiful mortal the world could offer in the form of Helen, the Spartan queen.

One small complication that didn't in any way perturb Aphrodite was that Helen was already married to Spartan king Melenaud. This didn't stop Paris who accepted Aphrodites offer crowning her the fairest of them all. Aphrodite drew on her powers to ensure Helen fell in love with Paris and left king Menelaus; this love triangle went on to become the catalyst for the Trojan war.

Aphrodite is a perfect deity to embrace if you have issues around self esteem, confidence and harnessing divine feminine energy. Aphrodite can show us how to practice decadent self care in order to raise our spiritual, physical, mental and emotional wellbeing. Also for setting better boundaries and higher expectations for our relationships. She can help us identify and move away from toxic relationships as a result of increased self love but also to work on existing relationships that may just need some nurturing to rekindle the passion and connection.

Aphrodite taught me to romanticise my life and to seek pleasure in the small things, a wonderful deity to work with for creative pursuits such as art, writing, poetry and creative projects.

Hekate

I can pinpoint the exact moment I discovered Hekate in one of my old journals. I look at that entry fondly and see it as another pivotal moment in my healing journey. I had been practicing and identified as a witch for a number of years, then around two years ago I started to identify and practice as a Wiccan starting out through observing the sabbaths.

In the past when I started my practice as a witch I felt confused in relation to the element of faith, my parents were atheists and didn't christen me or my brother to allow us to choose as adults which faith to take. I smile now remembering being somewhat aggrieved as a child in the main because of other children we knew having ostentatious christenings wearing big flouncy dresses. Looking back, I realise my mum has always held many pagan beliefs combined with a true natural earthiness, many of the Wiccan practices and observations seem to be second nature to her.

Working with deities is entirely optional for any witch, but for me it was key to me cleaning up my alcohol dependency. Through honouring and creating a devotional practice with a deity I found my faith and sense of being supported. I felt lost and angry over many of the decisions I had made over the course of my life, as I formed my relationship with Hekate many of our conversations began with me dropping to my knees sobbing, not asking for her to change anything but to help guide me to feeling better.

At this point I hadn't made the correlation with my alcohol consumption and my mental state, I just poured liquor on top of any issues that I had further fueling their power over me. Once I made the connection between my binge drinking and crippling anxiety and depression, long periods of sobriety made me start to see how good life could be, I began to feel joy and I recall early on talking to my mum of how I hadn't felt like this since my younger years, before drink or drugs had found a place in my life.

I was a high functioning alcoholic which was the same in my former drug addiction, I had the ability to hold down a full time high profile career whilst being a single mum, I won't say I did particularly well at both at times but very few people in my life had any idea what was going on behind closed doors, the binge drinking sessions I held with myself were two or three times a week consisting of anything from two to four bottles of red wine or prosecco or a large bottle of vodka or dark rum. The days that ensued following a session were like hell on earth, anxiety rattled within and ate away at me, I looked older and felt exhausted and ratty. I had made that age-old mistake of believing that alcohol helped me escape from my problems and allowed me to destress.

The irony is that through tackling my drinking problems most of the issues I had spent years harbouring healed and fell to the wayside without much effort, deeper issues that remained began to heal through counselling and my own accountability, however before we reached anywhere near that point Hekate was always by my side.

I identified with Hekate and her attempted suicide due to my own, Hekate was said to be raised from the dead by Artemis as an avenging spirit for injured women, she was a lover of solitude who was unwilling to sacrifice her independent nature for the sake of marriage, a situation I had not long found myself in where I had left my fiance, we had the ring, the dress, the veil, the venue, everything sorted.

Hekate hung out with the social outcasts and felt most comfortable and tolerant in the company that most of society would shun out of fear or misunderstanding, again this had mirrored my life seeking out people who did things differently or who didn't care what other people thought of them, my approach brought in both good and bad influences. Hekate is the protector of those who live on the edge or are oppressed, she has strong association with the moon which has always held such power over my own moods and behaviour, as it does for many of us. She is also the queen of dreams.

As a child and teen my dreams had always been somewhat prophetic, I dreamt of events before they occurred, I found out secrets or untruths within my dreams relating to relationships in my life, I had a visitation dream from my grandad Denis who had passed on, that dream was so real I could even smell the aftershave he always wore.

Throughout my hardcore drinking years my dreams all fell to the wayside, so much so I had forgotten I ever used to have them. It was only during periods of sobriety that I was able to predict forthcoming events or receive messages.

Once I started to get sober I received more psychic dreams than ever and on the regular, I will usually have one or two a week now, they have also increased over the months since I have been working on my podcast and this book.

My dreams developed to include numbers, I would wake up and that number would stick in my mind all day. I couldn't forget that number even if I tried for that whole day and they usually came in three or four digits.

I started to research each succession of numbers that came up and found myself either being guided, reassured that I was on the right track or notified of forthcoming events or areas of my life I needed to work on.

Recently I discovered that Hekate is said to have Iynges (divine messengers/angels) under her command. The angel number dreams began during my sobriety when my devotion to Hekate developed. Hekate is said to shine a torch to guide you in your dreams and she also shows us how to see or approach things differently.

Hekate is here to make us see what is hindering our growth and to leave what seems safe and familiar to journey to the darker unknown places within our soul. I had no ability to see any life without alcohol in it, the concept frightened me. I had such a reputation for being able to drink friends under the table and I was forever associated with prosecco, the irony is you could trade the glamorous bottles of prosecco for some of the cheapest bottles of cider and the truth remained the same. I was an alcoholic who didn't believe I could kick the habit or create a life where I could escape the vice like grip it had on me, if I am honest with you, getting clean from crack cocaine was a walk in the park because all I did was swap it out for alcohol, a substance that is so socially acceptable.

Hekate is said to show us that new beginnings aren't always easy, she is able to support us and shine the torch showing the way but also to help guide us when it comes to making big decisions.

Hekate is known by many names including the Goddess of Witchcraft, Queen of the Night, Goddess of Magick and Goddess of the Wilderness. She also holds the name of "The Distant One" yet she is said to always be at hand and to offer us the light of her torch to see which way to go, how to leave the past behind us and seek out the path to new beginnings. At first I wasn't sure how to start with honouring Hekate, I felt it out as I went along but in the main I prayed to her, addressed her when I carried out any spell work or rituals. I would light a simple tea light first thing in the morning and leave it on my altar wishing her a good morning and chatting with her about what I had on my mind or what intentions I had for that day.

Traditional offerings worshippers would make to Hekate include wine, beer, fruits (favoured by Hekate include pomegranate, grapes, dates) eggs, cheese and milk (goats cheese and milk is said to be preferred and Hekate has been depicted in imagery throughout history with a goats head), fish and meat. Hekate also welcomed honey (throughout time honey has been offered to the restless dead), olive oil, onion, sesame seeds, cardamom seeds, almonds, barley either as a grain or incorporated into baked goods, water, wine and incense.

Many baked goods such as bread and cakes. Specific cakes offered include Psammeta cake (a form of sacrificial cake), Magides which was a form of loaf and cake however we can substitute this with homemade bread and Amphiphon, a cheesecake that was surrounded by candles. It's good to leave baked goods out for wild creatures to enjoy on your deities behalf. Herbs and plants to offer up include sage, lavender, mugwort, roses and thyme.

Fire is another form of offering to Hekate, be it in the form of a tealight, candle, lantern (symbolic of Hekate lighting the way with her own lantern) and oil lamps. Also any form of fire you hold outside can be used to honour Hekate. Incense was often offered up for ouranic deities due to its smoke billowing up towards the heavens where the Greeks believed these gods and goddesses resided.

Offerings in Hellenic Greece were an essential part of their religion and culture in order to worship both the gods and spirits. There were two different forms of deities that the Hellenic Greeks would have made offerings to, chthonic and ouranic. Many of the different offerings listed above are a mixture of ouranic and chthonic offerings as Hekate straddled the two.

Chthonic relates to the gods and spirits of the underworld or the earth. Offerings to these particular deities were made without the devotee consuming any so as not to form any connection with the gods or spirits they were offered up to. These offerings were apotropaic in nature so offered up whole in a bid to avert evil/negative energy or miasma as it was referred to which translated loosely means pollution. Miasma is a term for a state of uncleanliness that renders you separate from ordinary society.

Chthonic rites would usually have been made at night outside the city walls, altars for chthonic rites honouring chthonic gods would be close to the ground and offerings would usually be buried or put in a bothos, which was an offering pit. As chthonic gods were underground, rites would involve kneeling with palms flat against the ground, it was believed that these gods had trouble hearing the prayers made so worshippers would strike or knock against the ground to get their attention.

Animals sacrificed for chthonic rites would be burnt whole and left complete for the underworld deities, black dogs were a common sacrifice in Hellenic Greece and one often made to Hekate, by sacrificing black dogs this was seen as a form of removing negative influences. Eggs, oil, garlic and onions were other common apotropaic offerings.

Ouranic means celestial so these offerings were made to any deity found above the surface of the earth, you consumed along with the god or spirits any food and drink you offered up in a bid to build connection with them. The food and drink would be blessed by the gods, a small part would be offered up to the gods or spirits first before the devotee would consume any, either by throwing the food into the fire or pouring it onto the earth. By throwing it into the fire the energy of the food could rise up to the heavens where the gods were believed to reside.

Incense was a particularly popular offering to make to the ouranic gods as the smoke rises, however it would be seen as pointless to use within chthonic offerings due to the gods not being able to experience and appreciate it from underground.

Ouranic rites would be held in daylight within the city walls and be of a more festive nature, ouranic altars would be three feet or higher up from ground level and during the rites worshippers would stand and hold their hands raised up to the sky. Animal sacrifices made during the rites would involve the animal blood being offered up to the gods and the meat being cooked and eaten by the people following on from the ritual. For most this would be the only time they would get to eat meat, none of the animal would be wasted. The animals sacrificed would be held in high regard and treated well before the rite being viewed as a gift from the gods.

Hekate was considered both chthonic and ouranic, she has dominance within the underworld but she also reigns over sky, sea and earth. Many altars discovered dating back to Hellenic Greece showed that Hekate was in the main worshipped as an ouranic goddess.

Some modern day witches opt not to make food or drink offerings believing it to be a waste of resources, however it has long been believed that metaphysically deities draw upon and use the energy and nourishment from the offerings made to assist their devotees within their lives and build a stronger connection. I regularly make offerings within my practice as I believe this nourishes my deities and is a small form of appreciation in comparison to the many blessings they bestow upon me.

You may want to provide offerings through the use of a libation bowl which you keep on your altar, this is simply a bowl that you feel deity worthy that you can leave any of your food offerings in. I use a pink vintage glass bowl but see what you feel drawn to use. I would recommend smoke cleansing your libation bowl with either incense or a smoke cleansing bundle and blessing and dedicating it to your deity before you add it to your altar. I leave full offerings for Hekate as that's how I started out within my practice however I like the idea of bringing the divine energy in from Hekate through sharing my offerings with her. If you are working with an ouranic deity or one that straddles the line between ouranic and chthonic you may opt to provide them an offering by leaving them the first piece of your food, you eat the second piece and leave them the last part. Historically this was always seen as a way to connect the two worlds and strengthen the connection to the gods.

Offerings that I make to Hekate on a daily basis are tealights and incense during daylight hours so more of an ouranic offering, for any other rituals or spell work I carry out I still draw upon the traditional offerings to Hekate. I offer up eggs, onions, garlic, grapes and different forms of fruits, almond soya milk, cardamom seeds are one of her favourite and flowers, I offer these up at night resulting in a combination of chthonic and ouranic offerings (the onions and garlic being apotropaic just in homage to how chthonic offerings would have been made). I usually leave any offerings I make on my altar for a few days, you can either bury libations once this time is up or pour them onto the ground. Some witches will even leave offerings they are removing from their altar at a crossroads at night when working with Hekate, however this isn't part of my own practice. I have had to throw away offerings at times as it isn't practical for me to bury every offering I make in my very small garden! You might have a compost heap you can use instead that would feed this back into nature.

Animal sacrifices would certainly not form part of most witches practice today, some witches will still offer up meat or the blood from it. I personally do not eat meat or consume most dairy products so do not offer these up within my rituals. I am not adverse to leaving animal bones that I have come across in nature on my altar for Hekate in homage to times of old where she would have animals offered up for both ouranic and chthonic sacrifices.

During rites held for both chthonic and ouranic deities the worshippers would often address the gods using their epithets. Epithets are used for all gods, both ouranic and chthonic deities, the most common example of using epithets I could give you would be Alexander the Great. The benefit of using epithets to worshippers then and even now for witches in their practice is when you are working with a specific god or goddess for their renowned powers and blessings in a certain area that you require assistance.

You may in your own devotion to your deity research the many epithets they hold and call upon them using an epithet most relevant to that you wish for assistance with in a bid to channel one of their specific powers.

During Hellenic rites chthonic deities would tradition-ally never have been called upon by their names in a bid to make the deity appear less scary and more help-ful – Hekate holds epithets such as Guardian, The Knowing One, Goddess of Death, Bearer of Love to less complimentary epithets such as Eater of Men's Hearts and Eater of Filth. The deities are bestowed with many and some epithets they held would often contradict others they were given.

There are traditional offerings that were made to Hekate, in Greek tradition suppers were left for Hekate on the dark moon at the crossroads, the cross-roads linked to Hekate are always said to have three ways and Hekate would face each path. The three ways may be an association to her ruling over earth, sky and the underworld but crossroads are also believed to be places where you are most likely to meet spirits and Hekate would offer her protection as a guardian.

Hekate is said to have two demon ghost hounds that accompanied and served her, as a result historically black dogs were often sacrificed for offerings. Hekate has many different forms of animal symbolism, she is depicted as having a lion, dog and horse's head but this differs across many texts and art.

Historically Hekate has been worshipped as a goddess of abundance and is said to bestow generous gifts upon those who show her devotion. Hekate had truly reigned supreme in my life helping me in ways beyond my wildest dreams.

The Morrigan

I had been honouring Hekate for a while working on a lot of my grief and pain. I had managed to hit longer periods of sobriety and whilst I wasn't there entirely I had managed to spend the most part of that year sober. It was sinking in how life was so much better this way. My finances had improved greatly however I was still struggling with managing my mental health which fed into my sobriety and my day job was really suffering. I could see that having spent the last six years working for the same company based at home had enabled me to keep drinking as I could hide my hangovers. I had too much freedom at this point and no need to show up fully sober.

I had a highly paid position and was unconvinced I could replicate this within a local job let alone stay sober on the daily and show up every day suited and booted. I felt stuck in a rut and after a time began drinking again, the cycle continued. I felt hopeless again as I began to spiral out of control once more. I remember Holly Whittaker, the author of Quit like a Woman stating that in order to get sober you need to create a life that you do not need to run away from. If I could sum up my reasons for excessively drinking it was always for escape.

This is when the Morrigan made herself known to me, her fierceness definitely made me feel nervous at first but again I was in awe of her, firstly her ability to help you look at the decay that is within your life and to transform it into something beyond your wildest dreams. I also understood that she would be the deity to work with if you needed to escape the quicksand that you found yourself stuck in within your life. I was sinking and no matter what I seemed to do I couldn't fully escape. The Morrigan doesn't suffer fools gladly and she would only work with me if I actually showed her I was prepared to do the work in order to change my life, she would transform it beyond anything I could ever imagine providing I carried out the actions.

I still wanted to work with Hekate but I felt that I had her permission to work with the Morrigan too, especially after discovering there are certain similarities between the Morrigan and Hekate. Both are generally classed as dark goddesses, a term applied to goddesses that have challenging aspects to them and links in respect of transformation and transition. Both deities are fearsome and never depicted as nice fluffy goddesses, I believe you only introduce yourself to both if you are not faint hearted but I also shy away from the term dark goddess as I believe in essence they are deities that highlight the shadow self in a bid for you to reach your true potential.

Both goddesses are also classed as triple goddesses so are shown as having three faces of mother, maiden and crone. The Morrigan is in essence said to be made up of three sister goddesses – Badb, Macha and Morrigu and each hold their own unique lore and powers.

The Morrigan is an Irish Celtic goddess of war, death, destruction and transformation. Daughter of one of the Tuatha De Danann, a pantheon of the first divine gods and goddesses of Ireland who fought for the country's possession. She is often depicted with crows or ravens on the battlefield, through this association she is said to demonstrate that life can be transformed through destruction. It is said that working with the Morrigan can lead us to achieve our wildest dreams and that through your devotion to her she won't fail you on what you are looking for. She will however ensure you carry out necessary shadow work and help you to confront your darkest demons. The Morrigan will make you work hard for what you want but the results will be beyond anything you ever expected with your own personal transitions and transformations that defy belief.

Who better to teach the art of transformation than a shapeshifter? the Morrigan was said to show up as a crow or raven, this is said to be her preferred form however she also shapeshifted into an eel, wolf and cow. The Morrigan often used her shapeshifting ability to influence people's fate.

I believe I have seen the Morrigan in the form of Morrigu, one of the three sisters and she is said to be how the Morrigan will first make herself known to you, this was through the most terrifying experience I have have ever had through seeing a crone in the corner of my bedroom, at the time I was working with the Morrigan but I had relapsed with alcohol and was dating someone unsuitable for me who happened to be in my bed the night of the sighting. It's tricky to differentiate this experience between a night terror or an apparition but I know it was her. As hard as I tried I couldn't scream, I didn't feel she would cause me harm but I could sense she wasn't impressed with me not being on track either.

The Morrigan is said to hold you accountable, if you fail to follow up on the actions or promises you have made in order to make your transition or if you fail repeatedly to pick up on any messages she is trying to give you she is known for giving you some short sharp shocks. You can avoid this however by restarting your devotional practices and heeding any messages that you pick up. She will give you another chance. It is said that through honouring the Morrigan properly she will never let you down.

As a dark goddess akin to Hekate many similar offerings can be made however I would consider adding black feathers to your altar symbolic of the crows and ravens seen alongside her on the battlefield or that she shapeshifted into. Milk is often left for the Morrigan, symbolic of the cow she shapeshifted into throughout her lore, also red wine and red foods symbolic of the blood shed on the battlefield.

The Morrigan holds many qualities that I deemed desirable, she was fiercely confident and powerful, she was renowned for using her sexuality to get what she wanted, something mostly taboo and discouraged in women however the Morrigan is said to embrace this.

She is a key goddess to work with for sacred sex magick, lore is that she lay with many men and had many children to unknown fathers however within her Celtic community this was nothing to be ashamed of as sex was such an important and revered part of their culture.

The Morrigan is said to often choose to work with divorced women or women who struggle to find the right partner, women who perhaps doubt their abilities and confidence yet are incredibly strong.

We only know of the Tuatha De Danann and their rituals and lore through the writings of Christian monks and the Roman military leaders as the Celts believed that through writing down their teachings they would no longer hold their magick.

Through carefully approaching the Morrigan and asking for her assistance she truly did give me the kick up the backside to take action, I got better at sobriety, I started counselling again seriously after the realisation I could no longer self-medicate with prosecco and on the whole I started showing up for myself day after day, I built on my practice as a witch until I was able to leave behind my day job to work for myself within the witchcraft industry. The Morrigan put the fear of the goddess in me. I had heard tales of her expecting you to keep your half of the bargain if you sought her out and I was not prepared to see how things could go if I messed around. The following day after approaching the Morrigan I received a letter notifying I would be paid back a large sum of money that I hadn't thought would be approved. Things really were beginning to change and I felt somewhat fearless once I started to honour the Morrigan.

Looking back it's funny how little we know is around the corner, these pivotal moments and one or two small decisions can lead to some of the most life changing events.

Nicneven

Nicneven sparked my interest when I first began to study Scottish folk magick as I built on work within my craft relating to ancestral magick. I first came across this Scottish deity within the book 'Folk Witchcraft' by Roger J Horne where he outlined the 'Conjuration of Nicneven'. an incantation chanted whilst dancing or walking in a circle around a fire in order to conjure this Scottish witch-queen.

I was even more intrigued when I learnt she has been described as the Scottish Hekate or 'Mother Witch of Scottish Peasantry'. She has links to the Germanic goddess Holda and Hel, Queen of the Underworld who is said to lead the Norse legend wild hunt.

Nicneven is said to derive from a Scottish gaelic surname Neachneohain which means daughters of the divine, also the gaelic name Nic an Neamhain which translates as 'daughter of frenzy' with frenzy referring to heaven which links directly to another name association to her - Nic Noamh that roughly translates to 'daughter of the saint'. It has long been debated which saint she is said to be related to but Brigid seems to be the name most bandied around.

Nicneven is described as the Queen of Elphame/Elfhame (elfin), Queen of the Fairies, Spirits and Strange Creatures, the Great Muckle Wallowa and Queen of the Unseelie Court of Alba (unseelie meaning wretched/unhappy and seelie means happy/pleasant).

She holds the title of crone goddess of Samhain and pumpkins and gourds hold particular relevance to honoring her on this night, they would be carved and used for protection and to illuminate the path for spirits' transition. On Nicnevens sacred night of Samhain she is said to answer petitions and grant wishes, you might wish to honour Nicneven during your Samhain feast and raise a toast to her. At Samhain druids would use the sabbath as an opportunity to resolve any disagreements they may have had with others, you might wish to call upon NicNeven to help you heal any relationships you have had conflict within. Write on a piece of paper the details of the disagreement and any anger you hold towards that individual. Call upon NicNeven for her power to bring peace and resolution to this relationship but also to destroy negative feelings and emotions that have arisen as a result. When you are ready, carefully light the piece of paper within your Samhain bonfire, cauldron or a heatproof bowl.

Nicneven is also honoured on November 11th as a result of the calendar shift that took place in 1752 where Samhain was moved forward by eleven days. It is said that Nicneven will ride out with her wild hunt between October 31st and November 11th.

Sir Walter Scott in 1831 described Nicneven and her wild hunt as follows

> 'a gigantic and malignant female, the Hecate of this mythology, who rode on the storm and marshalled the rambling host of wanderers under her grim banner. This hag (in all respects the reverse of the Mab or Titania of the Celtic creed) was called Nicneven in that later system which

blended the faith of the Celts and of the Goths on this subject. The great Scottish poet Dunbar has made a spirited description of this Hecate riding at the head of witches and good neighbours (fairies, namely) sorceresses and elves, indifferently, upon the ghostly eve of All-Hallow Mass'

Nicneven's wild hunt was said to consist of an unnamed fairy king who was said to always rule by her side, witches, spirits, and her court of unseelie fairies. White geese are sacred and symbolic to Nicneven and the sound of their cackling was said to herald her impending arrival. Overall her hunt was said to ride at Samhain, at dusk she would rise from the underworld, passing through the sea to enter and rise into the world of mortals and open the gate to the otherworld to allow spirits of the dead to cross into our realm. Her unseelie spirits and dark creatures would accompany her and between the hours of nine and ten at night she would allow herself to be visible to the eyes of mortals. Throughout lore Nicneven is also said to have led her hunt during storms and liminal times throughout the year.

There is some debate over the Cailleach and NicNeven being one and the same yet I like to view both as entirely separate beings, both deities do however have links to the beginning of winter and the night of Samhain. Both hold strong association to the harvest, seasons and power over the sea and land with the ability to transform into the land itself.

55

Nicnevin had the ability to shapeshift into different forms and move between different worlds, most frequently she would appear as a beautiful young woman who wore a long grey mantle and held a wand that could transform water into rocks and sea into solid land, or a crone who was often referred to by the name Habetrot or Gyre-Carling. Gyre is linked to the Norse word Gygr meaning Ogress and Carling is said to mean 'Crone' or 'Witch'.

Gyre-Carling or Habetrot, the hag form of Nicneven, held magical powers related to spinning, weaving and cloth making. Within Scottish superstition if you hadn't finished your knitting by New Years Eve she would steal it.

NicNeven is said to be a good deity to work with for any form of the craft as she is said to govern over the realism of magick and witchcraft. Call upon Nicneven for assistance with otherworldly travel (it is said she must be invoked to travel to the otherworld), divination skills, plant knowledge, weather magick (she is said to lead the wild hunt upon a storm), glamours, speaking with the dead (she can grant powers to talk to spirits from all realms), charms and protection when travelling at night.

It is said that if you spend a night on one of her crossroads, hills, or by the sea where land, sea and sky are all represented she will grant the specific magickal powers you require. You must bring offerings, arrive at dusk, invoke and wait for her presence. If she doesn't appear on the first night, keep returning to carry out the same for up to nine nights. If by the ninth night Nicneven hasn't arrived she isn't the right deity for you, should she arrive or send a spirit in her place state out loud exactly what you wish for and leave your offering right away. Leave calmly and peacefully for it is said if you run in fear you will forfeit that which you have asked for.

This is a section of 'The Witches Reel' which originates from 1591 and is laid out in Roger J Hornes book 'Folk Witchcraft'. Used as an incantation, you might decide to dance or walk around a fire nine times or simply cast your circle in your sacred space and dance carefully around a candle nine times in a bid to conjure the Scottish witch queen.

Conjuration of Nicneven

'Commer, go ye before!
Commer, go ye!
If ye will not go before
Commer, let me!
Ring-a-ring a widdershins,
a whirlin' skirlin' widdershins!
Commer, Carlin, Crone and Queen
Three times three!

It is said that as a Scottish deity her preference for offerings are whiskey, cider, mead or a good ale either homemade or store bought as long as its good quality.

Goddess Mode

Some of the most frequent questions I am asked as a result of my podcast are how can I find the right deity to work with? How can I work with them?. Most of my devotional practices are self-created with additional snippets of research and inspiration I have gathered along the way.

This ritual will help introduce you to your deity and allow you to see if they will reciprocate their interest in working with you. I recommend carrying this ritual out once you have exhausted all your research on this specific deity. Information may differ in relation to deities but you will soon start to see patterns in their accounts that seem more plausible to you. You may even find information that changes your mind on working with them and return to the drawing board in your search for your deity, this is a relationship that may last you a lifetime so do not begrudge the research period.

Once you are ready to carry out this ritual, preparation is key. I named this ritual goddess mode because we are going to treat and align ourselves with the deities as best we can as mere mortals. In early sobriety I found myself with more money to spend that was no longer used on wine or vodka. I began to take myself out and treat myself to flowers, candles, bath bombs and oils, lotions and potions and face masks. When you are healing from anything be it mental health issues, addiction, separation, grief or heartbreak I know that self-care gets bandied around a lot, but I cannot stress to you how much baths were such an important part of my toolkit especially as a means for grounding. When certain feelings began to take over or my addiction had me in a vice like grip these rituals were paramount.

When I felt the overwhelming urge to buy alcohol or dark feelings would overwhelm me I would quickly run a bath, light all the candles, start my meditation playlist, drop the bath bombs and oils in, reach for the face masks and get out some cosy clean pyjamas to wear following. I knew that once I had got out of my clothes and taken off my makeup there was no way I would be able to get ready and trek over to the shop across the road from me to buy prosecco.

If you are overwhelmed with feelings of wanting to call that toxic ex, former dealer, reach for the weed, bottle of vodka, binge eat a bag of donuts or any form of self sabotage this is one small part of your tool kit that will help take the urgency away and allow you to self soothe.

The element of water is heavily linked to our emotions and by bathing and crying at the same time our emotional system becomes able to flow more freely without being repressed or emotionally blocked.

For our goddess ritual I would recommend running yourself a bath with a new bath oil or bomb in a new scent, this is a new part of your healing journey so we want to start some new associations with you and your goddess. This bath should be one of the most important ones you have and signify the beginning of your relationship with your deity.

Perhaps buy yourself some beautiful seashell chocolates to bring in the element of the sea and the association with the water, add some of your moon water if you have previously made some (I recommend using moon water made at a new moon) add flower petals to your bath that are associated with your deity, you may wish to add almond milk akin to how the Egyptian goddesses bathed, drink elderflower juice or any decadent drink that you feel the deities and you will enjoy. Prepare your meditation music, use new scented candles, you may wish to buy new nightwear and body lotion to adorn yourself in following your bath. Try to bring new different elements into your bath routine, after all we are trying to heal and improve our life here!

Once in your glamorous bath, allow the warmth to seep into your bones, cry if you need to get anything out and allow your tears to flow into your bath water. We aren't holding these emotions back, this is where the pain gets stuck, allow yourself to honour these emotions and cry as much as you need to. I promise the day will come when those tears will dry up. If someone had said that to me in those days I would have wanted to roll my eyes and hold myself back from wanting to slap them but hear me out!

Once you have finished up in your bath you will hopefully feel lighter and have reached that delicious prune-like stage. Slather on some beautiful body oil or moisturiser, dress in your fresh pyjamas or any comfy clean cosy clothing, remember we are in goddess mode so a dab of scent might be good too. I associate Hekate with Chanel Black Noir, need I say anymore! You may even wish to find a new scent that you associate with your deity from this day forward so that once you wear it you embody the traits you associate with them.

Light candles on your altar or sacred space, I would definitely recommend burning incense to get you into a heady state. if you always cast a circle prior to any ritual prepare as you would normally. Now sit comfortably, we want to introduce ourselves to our deity through this meditation. I normally reach a meditative state through visualising a beautiful place far removed from my own environment or anywhere I have ever had the fortune to travel to. My place to journey to for many years has been a clearing deep within a green dewy jungle where there are large rocks and a natural pool in the centre. Take as long as you need to see where your mind wants to take you to and that brings you peace. When you are ready we are going to introduce ourselves to our deity. You may wish to prepare something before your ritual commences or allow the words to come to you freely within the moment.

Tailor your introduction according to your specific deity, their history and powers, you can't get this wrong so don't overthink it. You may wish to speak your introduction out loud or within your mind, however you feel called to. As an example I have outlined how first introductions could be worded.

'Hekate, Goddess of Witchcraft, Queen of the Night, I Carly Rose understand and have educated myself in relation to your legend, I find myself in awe of your strength, beauty, compassion for women and ability to light the way for those who seek transformation"

You now have the opportunity to talk to your deity and explain where you find yourself in your life currently. I would ensure your language is positive, you do not want to spend time moaning and grumbling at your deity, deliver the facts of where you find yourself on your healing journey and how you believe that their power can help you if they do decide to work with you. We are meeting with a powerful deity, be mindful of your manners and approach, they do not have to do anything for us.

Once you have spoken from your heart and feel your message is conveyed you may wish to finish off with something along the lines of "Hekate, I ask if you will please honour me with your support and guidance in order to heal". Be specific in asking them for their assistance and outlining how you require their support.

Now listen, sit in your meditative state in your sacred space within your mind for as long as you feel necessary, but do give it time. You might find that your deity has already made themselves known to you and you can see them in your witches eye (mind's eye), what are they wearing? how do they make themselves known to you? Are there specific colours that they are wearing? Are they holding any trinkets? Crystals? Do they have any symbolism on them anywhere? really look out for detail.

Do they speak to you? What's their body language saying? You might find that one specific word comes up for you or they may converse with you entirely, furnishing you with information you need to act on. Give adequate time in your meditative state following your request to hear what they have for you. You might even be surprised and another deity makes themselves known to you which might signify they are better suited to work with you or for your specific request.

One thing I am always conscious of within my practice or ritual is to never dismiss a deity from my circle within spell work, ritual or meditation. The audacity! Once your work is drawing to a close just let your deity know you are finishing up your work and thank them for joining you.

Once your meditation is complete I recommend reaching for your book of shadows or journal that you may have begun alongside reading this book and record everything you can from your meditation. What words and messages were relayed to you? If your god or goddess appeared, list everything you saw. If you notice any symbols, colours, trinkets or crystals around your deity look into their symbolism. Colours may pertain to the specific chakra you may need to unblock, specific crystals may need to help you with your healing. Following on from your ritual look into the symbolism of anything you see to gain insight to what your deity is trying to show you.

I would usually recommend leaving your deity offerings, especially for a first introduction and overall I find this is an important part of my practice. Through your research you should be able to discover that which your deity is partial to and tailor this accordingly.

If you didn't have the opportunity to meet your deity please don't worry, I recommend writing them a letter outlining all that you want to convey, what you like about them and what you would like their help with. Just because they didn't make themselves known to you doesn't mean to say they haven't heard your call and aren't getting to work on your request. I would recommend you leave this letter under your pillow for the following week and see what dreams come to light. Look at any messages you pick up over the course of the week or synchronicities that may occur that you feel are linked to them. You may be trying to converse with Persephone and keep seeing images of pomegranates! Jot down any messages you receive, any signs and dreams that you have that relate to your deity. Observe any changes in your life that you feel they may have assisted with, also monitor how you feel, are you feeling fearless like the Morrigan? a better ability to adapt like Persephone?

Going forward you may wish to use this ritual when you wish to converse with your deity on a grander scale. On a daily basis I will light both Hekate and the Morrigan a tea light at my altar in the morning and greet them. I like to tell them what I appreciate in them and what is happening in my life for that day. At times I ask them if they might help me with their strength or confidence or to intervene in a specific way if they see fit. Show up daily in little ways for them and before you know it they will do the same for you.

Magick

At the heart of my practice has been spell work. I firmly believe you do not need to possess all the tools or elements for a spell nor should you shy away from carrying out spell work due to confidence. I will never forget reading a section of the book 'Wicca' by Scott Cunningham that emboldened me with a similar message. In a nutshell he advises to try not to be too serious or scared to inadvertently make a mistake when carrying out your rituals and if something does go wrong he is sure the deities have a sense of humour. To summarise, as long as your heart is in it, your intention is pure, I believe you can make your intentions happen. The old adage of if you can see it in your mind you can hold it in your hand.

We can visualise an element of a spell if we cannot obtain it, we can utilise a white candle in place of any other colour candle and still obtain the same result. After all, hundreds of years ago witches would have used candles made from animal tallow without the luxury of having it a specific colour!

When it comes to spell or ritual work it involves a lot of high energy so you need to feel up to it mentally and physically. Better to embark on any spell work when you haven't eaten for a good few hours, spiritually it is said to be easier to connect to the divine when you aren't full up on food. Spell or ritual work can really drain you so eating a meal or snack afterwards can help to restore your depleted energies.

I tend to carve out some quality time to do any spell or ritual work I have planned, there are regular rituals I tend to carry out relating to the full and new moon and I often have particular spell work I wish to carry out that pertains to current circumstances in my life. I have to feel aligned with a spell before I decide to embark on it, I also try to source as many of the items required for the spell as I believe this conveys to the divine/my deity that I am serious about this spell, but again if I cannot get hold of a specific item I have no qualms in replacing it with another that's relevant or visualising an element in my mind if needs be.

I also enjoy creating my own bespoke spells, I truly believe this can hold even more power because this comes from your heart. You can easily look up herbs and plants and ascertain what their magickal proper- ties are and use them accordingly. You also have free reign over what they symbolise to you. An example I can give you is that some witches believe red candles should be used for passion so perhaps used in a spell to invoke a passionate affair but others might believe it stands for true love and represents the heart. It varies from witch to witch dependent on your personal associations.

One thing I am very passionate about within my spell work is using herbs that are native to where I live. I feel this is important as it helps me connect to the land. You may opt to grow your own herbs that you can use within your practice, as a UK based witch I swear by growing common garden sage, rosemary, mint, thyme, lemon balm and lavender and these give me the basics for many spells but also wonderful ingredients for teas, smoke cleansing bundles and general herbal remedies.

Sage is great for spell work relating to purification, wisdom, emotional strength, wishes and protection. Grown in a garden it is said to bring in success and abundance and it's a great hardy herb that can grow and prosper in most gardens in pots or the ground and will come back year after year. It's sometimes listed as a moon herb and has links to Jupiter and Zeus, also the wisdom of the crone. The Romans believed it helped to quicken the senses and memory.

Sage can be used within spell work to temper the results with wisdom, you can burn sage when you need to cleanse/purify and also if you need wisdom to make a difficult decision. It's ideal for use in spellwork to release unwanted desires.

You can add fresh sage leaves to boiling water to create a tea to help with grounding, anxiety and a bloated stomach, alternatively allow the tea to cool and drink to soothe a sore throat or problems of the throat. Sage has antibiotic agents that create its healing properties, as an anti-inflammatory you can apply it to relieve bites and stings.

Rosemary is another easy herb to grow that thrives in the ground or pots and will keep growing year on year, it can last for up to thirty years! The Egyptians used it within their burial rituals and it was brought to England by the Romans, it's great to use in spell work pertaining to cleansing, concentration, memory, protection, warding off evil spirits, healing, dream magick, protection against nightmares, sleep, spell breaking rituals and rejuvenating the mind and aura.

Rosemary is said to be one of the oldest herbs used for incense, when burnt it holds powerful cleansing and purifying vibrations. It's great to burn whilst reading or studying as it is said to help with memory and concentration, place rosemary under your pillow to assist with sleep and protection from bad nightmares. Fresh rosemary added to boiling water to create tea is great for digestion and to help keep your gut happy, also to drink if you are weaning yourself off caffeine or stimulants. Rosemary has links to both the sun and the moon and is said to be linked to the deities Aphrodite, Hebe and Persephone.

Mint is good to use in spell work for wealth, prosperity, luck, energy, renewal, healing, divination and communication. It's linked to deities such as Hekate, Hades and most notoriously Persephone. Persephone discovered Hades having an affair with a river nymph called Minthe, Persephone consumed with rage sought out revenge on the nymph and stepped on her using all her strength. The nymph survived Persephone's attack yet was transformed into a mint plant so each time Persephone stepped on her the scent of mint was released.

Mint is a wonderful herb to work with for abundance and money spells, you might want to add a few leaves to your wallet to bring in more money or drink mint tea before you embark on any divination work as it's said to increase psychic visions.

The word thyme comes from the Greek meaning to fumigate and was used by the Greeks within their temples to ward off negativity and to purify the environment. Greek soldiers were known to have massaged with thyme oil or to add thyme to their bath water to enhance their personal courage. They used it to adorn their temples and homes and women wore it within their hair. The Egyptians used thyme within their embalming practices and throughout the middle ages it was used to ward off nightmares by placing it under pillows before sleep, women would embroider sprigs of thyme into the attire of their knights and warriors for bravery and courage.

Throughout Europe it was historically placed on top of coffins to assure safe passage into the next life. During the black death millions used thyme for protection and as relief either through wearing it as a posie or using it for poultices that were applied to open wounds. It has some strong historical usage but to this day is still renowned for being used in spell work for courage, strength and protection from evil.

Thyme can be used within spell work for happiness, healing, independence, loyalty, luck and health. It's a popular herb of the fae and it is said that they love to dance around thyme in the garden. A pagan belief was that if the fae had any part in any of your objects going missing you could, on the night of a full moon leave them an offering of thyme along with something sweet to eat and a kindly polite request for them to help you find said lost item. If you are lucky they may be happy to help you with the search or return of the item as a result.

Thyme growing in your garden is said to bring positive energy to your home, wear it upon your person to protect you from evil spells and to fuel your own personal courage and strength. You might opt to add thyme leaves to your bath akin to how the Greek soldiers did in a bid to increase confidence, courage and boldness. Add fresh thyme and marjoram as a combination in your bath whilst in your early deep healing as it is said to help remove sorrowful negative feelings. Place thyme under your pillow for a restful night's sleep as they would have within the middle ages. Add thyme bundles to spell work for any work around transitions within your life and leaving the past behind.

Tea made from fresh thyme leaves is great as a remedy for upset stomachs but also for throat issues as its antiseptic and antifungal. It can assist you drunk as a tea if you are having problems with your cough reflex or breathing problems during illness. Brew it up as a tea and allow it to cool and it becomes a great remedy for athlete's foot!

Thyme is best grown in a sunny spot, it's pretty hardy and can handle a deep freeze so much so it's often found growing wild in the Scottish highlands. It has associations with Aries, Mars and Freya, the element of water and the planet Venus.

Lemon balm has to be one of my favourites, I associate it with the heart and find it great to brew up as a tea using fresh leaves to drink to aid a broken heart and loss. The scent of the leaves alone are said to lift melancholy and as a tea it's also great for anxiety and works as a mild sedative, so great to sip on to ensure a good night's sleep.

You can create a poultice using lemon balm leaves that have been ground down using a mortar and pestle, add a small amount of water to blend it all together into a balm and apply directly to wounds or stings to benefit from its healing qualities. Lemon balm was historically used as a balm following surgery to ensure incisions wouldn't become infected. During the middle ages it was placed throughout the home to ensure protection and harmony. The Romans and Greeks associated the herb with wealth due to the bees' strong attraction to it. It has some of the same chemicals that are in bee pheromones and as a result beekeepers use a compound of crushed leaves to attract worker bees to new hives.

Lemon balm is great to use within moon rituals as it has heavy association with the moon, within spell work its ideal for work pertaining to love, healing, release, fertility, friendship, success, emotions and harmony.

Lemon balm grows rapidly and spreads in rich well drained soil in a sunny spot, it requires little tlc but likes good drainage. It is linked to the deities Diana, Artemis, Pluto and Venus.

Lavender is another one of my faves and I love to use it within kitchen magick. One of my favourite days ever involved a picnic at Lammas with my daughter

Amelie and best friend Hannah at the screaming woods in Pluckley. We feasted on lavender and lemon cake amongst other homemade treats and drove back home after. It was a balmy hot summer night and the biggest moon I have ever seen was in the sky. It felt truly magickal. Add crushed sprigs of lavender to shortbread, cakes, cookies, or infuse in cream or lavender for an absolute culinary delight. Not too much though to avoid that soap taste!

Lavender is perfect to use as a natural remedy for insomnia, depression, irritability, anxiety, fatigue and stress. You can burn it to give you better clarity, psychic insight for your dreams, add to any calming baths before you embark on any ritual work or create a smoke cleansing bundle using it to burn for purification. Use lavender in spell work for manifesting, prosperity, good luck, love, peace, happiness, and communication. It is antifungal, antiseptic and antibacterial and can be used for burns, wounds and to relieve pain and inflammation. As with the lemon balm, crush in a pestle and mortar and mix to a balm and apply.

Lavender can be used as a tea which is somewhat an acquired taste, you don't need to add much lavender to it and you may wish to add some honey or lemon to get the taste to your liking but a perfect tonic for anxiety and to assist sleep but also for its anti-inflammatory benefits.

It has association with the element of air and the deities Artemis, Boreas, Eos and Iris. I work with English lavender, this tends to be one of the herbs that I am a bit useless at growing but overall it requires good drainage as it tends to survive better if watered sparingly, I can be an overkeen waterer at times! It's fairly tolerant of low temperatures and enjoys lots of sunshine. The one herb I buy year in year out but always worth it.

All of these six herbs are easy to purchase and grow. I am an advocate of growing herbs that you can use in your craft, be it in a sprawling acreage of land, a small patio garden like mine in pots, a balcony or even a windowsill. Let nothing stop you but this will provide you with six herbs that you can have at hand to use within your practice for pretty much every eventuality. The magick lies not only within the work you do using the herbs but the process of growing and nurturing them too, feeling the connection to the land and living things. There is nothing better than that within my practice and I find it incredibly rewarding. Spells that require ingredients that are commonplace within the depths of another country and not native to my home lands are not for me. I like to consider and replicate how a hedge witch might have worked within her practice in days of old.

Before I start any of my magickal workings I like to let fellow members of my household know I am not to be disturbed, fortunately I am out of the broom cupboard so everyone knows I am off to conjure something up!

I start off by running a soothing candle lit bath, I have on occasion added to my bath fresh herbs from my garden. I have used mint (protection, healing, happiness), rosemary (purification, banishing, protection) and sage (cleansing and purification). I like to have a bath purely by low candle light as in essence I am preparing to connect with the divine and enter into liminal space and time.

Once I have finished with my bath I will dress in comfortable light clothing, I keep the lighting low in my bedroom and light candles at my altar and incense sticks. Dragons blood is my favourite and I recently discovered this is the best form of incense for success within any magickal workings you may be carrying out, it also has strong protection properties. Overall it is said that incense can actually lift your mood, it certainly has this effect on me but by burning incense my brain over the course of time now understands and associates it with the beginning of work pertaining to my craft.

I spend a lot of time preparing for the work I have at hand. I collect any tools, spell books or items I need for a spell. My sacred space is within my bedroom. I sit on a Moroccan style rug facing my altar, a beautiful French style chest of drawers that has large glass handles. The items on my altar have been collected over the course of time and each one has a real connection with me. I am yet to find myself an athame or a wand to add to my altar as I still haven't found the right one for me, I am confident one will cross my path at the right divine time.

My altar comprises of many candles in beautiful rose quartz holders (fire element), a chalice which is actually a Scottish white milk glass bonbon jar from the 1900's that I purchased in Scotland from an small antiques store (water element), incense sticks (air element), a small French porcelain vintage jam dish full of salt (earth element), a glass jar full of spell candles, tarot and oracle cards, a small cauldron which I use in spell work for burning or combining spell ingredients, a jar of moon water taken from either the last full or new moon dependent on my intentions/needs, plants (I currently have a plant on my altar that I bought at Ostara, many Wiccans will add a new plant to their altar at this time. I usually name all my plants), an abalone shell which contains sage wraps, crystals in a cup and saucer that I have used for tasseography (tea leaf reading) and large pieces of rose quartz (my favourite crystal), a selenite tower and smoky quartz.

I opt to cast a circle for any spell or ritual work that I do; however not all witches will prepare in this way. I believe that by casting a circle I am creating my own protected space, I am then in a liminal space so 'betwixt and between', a phrase witches often use for a place in-between worlds. By casting a circle I can contain the high energy that I generate within and keep any negative energies or spirits on the outside.

I begin by mixing some of the salt from my altar into my chalice of water (I use my fingers from my dominant hand however you can use your athame). Starting facing east (air element) I begin to flick the combined water and salt from my fingers as I move deosil (clockwise) from where I stand facing east, round to south (fire element), then to west (air element) through to north (earth element).

As I do this I envisage a bright white light circling around me and the area I am working in, almost like a large white halo or hula hoop of protection. Once I come back to where I started in the east I take a lighted incense stick or sage bundle and move again from the east in a clockwise direction round to south (fire element), then to west (air element) and round to north (earth element). Whilst I am doing this I hold the incense or sage within my dominant hand for magick, with my other hand I waft the smoke around using a large feather I have (air element) envisioning my circle building in its strength and power.

Returning back to my position facing east I now begin the grounding process, standing with my eyes closed and my feet firmly against the ground hip width apart I envisage strong roots growing out of the bottom of my feet into the ground beneath me, beneath the foundations of my home into the earthy soil, I envisage these roots holding me up firmly. Once I feel planted in the earth I begin to visualise hot white light coming through these roots deep in the earth beneath my home making its way into my feet, the heat feels comforting and warm and gradually filters its way up through my legs into my thighs into my groin area and up through my stomach, I envisage it filling up all of my body with beautiful warm white light moving up into my heart, my chest, up into my shoulders and out into my arms right down to the tips of my fingers. This light then makes its way up my neck into my head and then up and out through the top of my crown beaming up into the sky.

Once I feel this light has run its course fully through all of me I gradually open my eyes, if you work with a deity you may wish to call upon them at this point to watch over you and assist you within your work. Hekate and the Morrigan are the two deities I opt to work with in the main, I will normally invite both politely to join me saying something along the lines of

"Hekate, I ask if you will watch over me whilst I carry out my work".

I then lift my right arm up as I am facing east and speak the following words, "I invite the element of air as I cast my circle", I then move again in a clockwise direction to south saying "I invite the element of fire as I cast my circle". I move around and do the same at west for the element of water and finish up at north for earth. I will then reach my right hand up to the sky and say "I invite the element of spirit as I cast my circle" then I will say "as above" and then I will point down to the ground and say "so below".

I will then go on to carry out any ritual or spell work within this space. When I first started out casting my circle I would often forget to bring certain items into my circle. Should you ever need to exit your circle albeit briefly it is possible to cut a doorway within your circle. Using an athame or again your dominant magick hand, envisage cutting a door tall and wide enough for you to exit and enter into your circle. Once I have visualised cutting the shape of a door I put my hand out to turn an imaginary door handle and step out of my circle. I then visualise and act out as though I am closing the door behind me in a bid to keep the energy withheld. I will quickly locate anything I need, return to my visualised door, open the handle and step back into my circle closing the door behind me.

Once I have carried out any magick within my circle I will often utilise the high energy within to carry out a tarot or oracle card reading, sometimes I might ask my cards questions that tie in with the spell work I have carried out.

Once I am perfectly satisfied with my work it's key for me to close my circle using the same amount of energy I invested to cast it. Starting again facing east I will say "I thank the element of air and release you from this circle", this time I move round widdershins (anti-clockwise) round to north, the element of earth and thank and release each element until I return to my starting point facing east. I then state "the circle is now closed", I make sure to thank my deities for joining me for the work I am carrying out and I let them know I am closing things up but they are welcome to leave whenever they see fit.

Spell and ritual work can be very tiring so I tend to carry it out late at night and not long before I am due to get off to bed. I also find that sleeping on any spell or ritual work I have carried out can sometimes offer up some interesting dreams and answers that relate to my magick work.

Book of Shadows

One of the most transformative tools within my healing journey became journaling and documenting my witchcraft journey through the use of a grimoire and book of shadows.

In essence a grimoire is a form of magickal encyclopedia containing all your witchcraft generals, somewhere you might wish to list topics such as colour magick correspondences, magickal hours to work with, magickal days of the week and their relevance to cast certain spells, the moon phases and work to carry out in accordance with each, spells, herbs, plants, crystals and their uses and overall anything relating to your witchcraft journey you have picked up and wish to note.

Your book of shadows is used to outline your findings or thoughts, a personal documentation of your journey with the craft so you may wish to outline rituals you carried out, spell work, dreams that you have had, shadow work you have worked through, desires you are manifesting and any experiences that are specific to your witchcraft path.

It is not essential to possess both books and some witches will combine the two. Grimoires date back centuries to France where they would have originally been known as a grammaire. It was only during the 1400's when printing houses started that they were printed on a wider scale and fell into the hands of more individuals. The Roman Catholic inquisition feared these works falling into the mainstream as their ideas didn't align with many of their beliefs, if caught with any magickal book you could be disciplined or put to death. As a result, magickal books of this kind were secreted away with only the very daring taking the risk to own them. Grimoires written in Latin continued to circulate up to the 1800's despite other works progressing to being printed in the French language. The term 'It is like a grimoire to me' was coined as a figure of speech to indicate how difficult these books were to read and interpret.

The term book of shadows originates from Gerald Gardner's own grimoire created during the late 1940's and early 1950's. Gardner was an English Wiccan who brought Wicca to the forefront with his work as an author and founder of Gardnerian Wicca. Doreen Valiente joined Gardner's Bricket Wood Coven in 1953 and was quickly appointed High Priestess . Valiente realised much of the grimoire Gardner had created drew upon much of occultist Aleister Crowley's work, an English occultist. In 1946 Gardner had purchased from Crowley's order, Ordo Templi Orientis, the workings and permission to carry out their rituals. Gardner's work also contained freemasonry rituals and references to the book of 'Aradia, or the Gospel of the Witches' written by Charles Godfrey Leyland and published in 1899. This book is said to document the rituals and beliefs of an Italian pagan witch group, however controversially many historians argue the sacred text this book was based on never previously existed. Despite this 'Aradia, or the Gospel of the Witches' did become an important part of the development of Wicca. Gardner's book had been given a few names before he settled on 'Book of Shadows'. Valiente believes he decided on the title following the sight of an article under the same name within an occult magazine.

Initially there was some resistance from members of Gardner's coven for his 'Book of Shadows' to be printed. Traditionally a book of shadows would have been destroyed upon the death of a witch, mainly to ensure no one discovered the individual had been one. Many claim Gardner's 'Book of Shadows' to be disjointed and jumbled in its layout and it was theorised this was in fact deliberate so the uninitiated could not understand its teachings.

Despite Gardner's 'Book of Shadows' being created in a time when witchcraft laws were no longer relevant, he still included guidance for a witch on what they should do if they happened to find themself on trial and tortured for witchcraft. Gardner claimed that this was of historical origin yet it was the first time in history that witches had been allowed to write anything along those lines without being incriminated for it.

Traditionally and to this day many covens still work to Gardner's original rituals and traditions, they will often hold only one book of shadows that the High Priestess will keep secret and safe. It's commonplace today for many modern witches to work in solitary and create their own book of shadows or grimoire to work from.

Again you may choose to keep your own grimoire and book of shadows or you might intend on a merge of the two. Constructing your own is a chance to draw upon your unique creative skills, you only have to look online at Pinterest or Instagram to see beautiful examples created by other witches. One thing I would like to stress that troubled me for a while and led to me procrastinating on the start of my own grimoire and book of shadows was feeling intimidated by how beautifully illustrated many other witches magick books were, once I finally got on and started I found having both books valuable to my craft and very sacred to me no matter how artistic they looked!.

I found a beautiful black spiral bound art sketch book for the purpose of my grimoire; it has a black satin ribbon to tie the book shut on one side. You may wish to start out with an index in both your book of shadows and grimoire by leaving a few pages free at either the front or back of your book and list page numbers and topics as you go along for quick and easy reference.

You may wish to add specific topics to your grimoire and/or book of shadows such as the different types of crystals and their properties, herbs and their properties, the elements and how to work with them, different types of witches and magick (green, sea, kitchen, hedge, weather, storm, cosmic, bone, death magick etc.), divination (tarot, runes, palmistry, tea leaf reading, pendulums, throwing bones etc.), moon phases, new and full moon rituals, making sun or moon water and its different uses, deities and specific information relating to them such as their history, favoured offerings, how best to work with them, astrology, animal symbolism, colour magick, candle magick, spells, rituals, chants, different forms of magick (white, grey, black), the history of witchcraft, knot magick, recipes (especially for witches who use cooking and baking in their craft), spell bags, talismans, plant identification, spirit work, altar tools and their symbolism/uses, sigils and their individual meanings, witchcraft history, planets and their relation to mythology and magick,

Some witches like to purchase a beautiful note or art book to use for their grimoire or book of shadows. You may decide to draw upon your creativity and construct your own notebook through book binding or making your own paper (you could include herbs or flower petals within the pages that magical properties assist with secrecy or protection, you might opt to use flowers to dye the pages, you could even add spell ashes to draw upon your previous spell work and enhance the books magick) you may opt to give your book an old style look through tea staining paper or marbling. You might add your own illustrations relating to botanical information or crystals and so on, or favour photographs you have taken of them instead, you might cut out pictures from magazines or Pinterest. I have stuck envelopes within the back of my book of shadows to store small items, you could add pressed flowers, dried herbs, anything you wish to store within these. You can find and stick pretty envelopes into your book or even create your own using pretty paper and washi tape. The more energy you put into the creation of your magickal books, the more energy and connection it will hold.

Some witches opt to place a protective curse over their magick books or cast spells across them for secrecy or protection. For the first page you may wish to include some form of dedication – I have written my full name, date of birth and date I have started this particular book of shadows and I will later document the date it was completed.

You might wish to add a form of blessing for your book of shadows or grimoire, for example, you could use a poem that you like or have penned. I have written a small statement in my book of shadows pledging my devotion to my goddesses Hekate and the Morrigan and asking them to guide and support me within my craft. I have requested if they can help ensure my book of shadows is protected and secret from anyone but me. If you are Wiccan you may wish to add and use the Wiccan Rede or the Wiccan prayer to Lord and Lady Wicca.

Within my book of shadows I like to include personal findings, outline sabbaths from the Wiccan wheel of the year, how I celebrated and with whom, which spell work or rituals I carried and any recipes associated with the sabbath that I tried, incorporating photographs wherever I can. I plan and document rituals or spell work I have personally created, plans I have in regards to full or new moons and that which I want to release from my life and manifest.

I have a bucket list for witchy places I would like to visit, hobbies I would like to carry out relating to my craft - you may wish to visit beautiful woods or a forest and find a piece of wood to craft your own wand, you may decide to work on pottery to create your own libation bowl or if you work with the fae, you might wish to document how you will create a tiny fairy garden for them to enjoy.

I also list witchcraft books I have read and others I would like to, I document any information that I feel is of importance to me and my craft and the source and page within that specific book I found the information so I can reference it if I need to.

The back of my book of shadows gets the most use as I document my dreams and their relevance to my current circumstances in detail, I also document any synchronicities I may have experienced, for example I had a period in my life where I continuously saw butterflies, not just in real life but also on social media at a time where my life was in dramatic transformation. I also had a period when I saw grasshoppers, both in my garden (I live by the sea with no real land!) and kept pulling the grasshopper card from my animal oracle deck that symbolised I needed to let go of the past and take the leap in relation to my witchcraft work after a time of doubting myself and my abilities.

It's also useful to document any tarot, oracle card or psychic readings that you may have, through recording your dreams, synchronicities and divination you can use this as a guide for your present situation in life but also for looking back at a later date to see how these messages from spirit have helped you towards your current circumstances.

Journaling has always been a key part of working with my subconscious mind, I began keeping a diary in my late childhood years after being gifted a series of padlock teddy bear diaries from Father Christmas, however I really fell in love with journaling after visiting Catford Cinema in south London with my first real boyfriend (the same one I later went on to share a crack cocaine addiction, so this relationship did start out somewhat sweet and innocent). We watched Bridget's antics and the whole way through the film I couldn't wait to get my hands on my own beautiful hardback journal and start jotting down my own.

The day following watching that film I found myself in a well-known British stationery shop in London making the decision on which beautiful notebook would become my very own Bridget Jones style diary. I settled on a white book with lipstick kisses on it with a red satin tie on the side to keep it closed. I wrote everything into that book but what I built on was a love of writing that has never left me.

Journaling is a truly transformational process, I owe a big part of my recovery from both addiction and codependency to a journaling practice. One of the greatest medicines for my anxiety and depression proved to be writing Morning Pages following on from reading 'The Artist's Way' by Julia Cameron. In the book Cameron advises you to write three full pages first thing on rising in the morning. So before you check your phone, start on breakfast and the like you just get everything out onto the page, this isn't a case of writing your best work its exorcising your niggles and whines, concerns or issues you may be dealing with, your morning pages can be writing on anything you want with the sheer objective of uncovering your thoughts.

These thoughts may come across as negative, whiny, fragmented, distorted and completely random. I found that this emptied the contents of my sad, anxious brain onto the page and before I knew it I was writing on ways that I could solve these issues. Creative ideas would come to me including many that led to this book's content.

Although Cameron created the morning pages as a tool for creatives to assist with creative recovery I found this was one of the most integral parts that kept me from self sabotaging again as I documented the worst of my thoughts and worked through them. It was a ritual I have shown up to everyday even if I felt I had nothing to write, before long something would come to the surface for me to sift through. Other times a solution might come to me later on in the day to issues I had outlined in my morning pages.

Journaling has recently led me to more intense shadow work such as working on what my inner child needs. If you are a recovering addict like me you may be more than familiar with how your inner child plays out. During early recovery mine showed up at around six years of age, think Angelica from Rugrats in appearance and nature and a pretty good similarity to how I looked around that age. My inner child now shows up slightly more mature at around thirteen yet still a force to be reckoned with.

Shadow Work

The most transformational soul wrenching yet transformational part of the healing process, Shadow work.

The process of uncovering your wounds, behaviour and triggers and bringing them into the light. I avoided shadow work at all costs, I relived the same experiences under different guises again and again relating to relationships, money, addiction and self-destructive behaviour convinced that would be easier than finally facing my shadow and listening to what little me, or rather my inner child wanted to say.

Shadow work appeared to be too murky an activity to delve into, a process I didn't believe I had the mental capacity or strength to unravel in a bid to digest my demons and trauma. After finally surrendering and working through it I am convinced you can find yourself feeling incredibly uplifted following shadow work, as though a huge burden has been lifted from your shoulders.

Let me reassure you by saying that my former self is the queen of procrastination. Why do something today if you can put it off till next week? That was the motto

I lived by. I put off everything, I couldn't even phone a utility company about a bill without the depths of fear coming over me let alone get alone tackle shadow work. Any time accountability came up for me I would leg it to my local again to buy bottles of prosecco.

So the way I got started and the most powerful task I ever carried out was writing a list of every single event or memory across my lifetime that made me feel serious discomfort, want to vomit at the embarrassment of or thoughts that caused me serious mental pain. I sat in my bed with candles lit late at night and wrote down every single memory going back to my childhood. I documented what happened, exactly how I saw the event, the feelings I experienced and how I believe it had affected me.

The more I wrote, the more further traumatic uncomfortable events came to mind. I wrote and wrote into my book of shadows until my hands were numb and my eyes were sore through floods of tears. But my heart started to feel lighter throughout the process, I wrote down events that no one other than me was even aware of. I must add none of it was fluffy but delved into my drug and alcohol addiction, being cheated on, lied to, sexually abused, physically abused, betrayed. The list was pages long and went into gut wrenching detail.

As I wrote that list I could uncover more and more in relation to the patterns I had repeated over and over again, I noted how in romantic relationships I wrote about I could see how every partner I had held exactly the same toxic traits and behaviour, I noticed my own toxic traits and red flags and repeated responses, how

I sought out and thrived off the same chaos. Most importantly I realised how my shadow had distorted many of my thoughts, Marianne Williamson explains this best in her book 'The Shadows Effect'

'The shadow is your own thinking turned in the wrong direction. It is your self-hatred masquerading as self-love. Your shadow is as intelligent as you are, because it is your own intelligence co-opted for fear's purposes. It has all the attributes of life, because it has attached itself to your life. And like all life, it seeks to preserve itself'

I realised how an untended emotional wound and trauma at the age of twelve had been the start of my abandonment issues. We start to demonstrate behaviour as a result of the trauma wound and we can subsequently attract further traumatic events but also distort our perception of these events. By bringing these trauma's into the light we start to remove their power over us, we can then start to heal our emotional inner child that has been long abandoned. I could visualise my inner child as thirteen years old, she regularly showed up in my adult life in the form of anger similar to that I felt as a teenager, feeling ignored and unheard. She would desperately push for my attention and I could feel her trying to push me off course in the form of self-sabotage.

The Wounded Witch

- People pleases and says yes to doing things they don't want to do

- Feels stuck within their life and unable to get to where they want to be
- Waits or relies on someone else to save them – a parent, friend or romantic partner
- Remains in toxic relationships as they are concerned about the work involved in having to leave
- Attracts emotionally unavailable people
- Struggles to leave their comfort zone to take on new tasks or activities
- Hoards feelings, people, emotions and struggles to let them go
- Struggles to commit or trust, looks for excuses not to trust people
- Inability to trust themselves, unforgiving to themselves or work to rigid perfectionism
- Poor sense of identity
- Easily offended and hurt
- Represses emotions or experiences irrational emotional outbursts
- Low self-worth
- Fears being vulnerable or being hurt
- Enjoys drama or conflict
- Fails to set boundaries within relationships
- Experiences the same issues or red flags within new relationships or events repeatedly
- Disassociates from emotional trauma/events
- Fails to tackle internal work in order to heal
- Associates with other traumatised individuals
- Discusses their issues repeatedly but fails to take action on healing them
- Consistently seeks external validation
- Seeks permission from others for personal decisions

- Struggles to accept individuals disagreeing with them
- Seeks approval for plans/goals/desires
- Jumps from relationship to relationship to avoid the status of single
- Dislikes being alone, fear of being 'left out'
- Threatens to leave often in relationships for any response
- Over apologises or often feels overly guilty
- Struggles to ask for support or asks for too much without trying to help themselves
- Uses guilt to manipulate
- Allows others perceptions of you to heavily affect your mood

———————— ◆◇◆ ————————

It's no mean feat to tackle your shadow and I recommend starting this process at a time that you feel mentally prepared to take on the work, only you will know when you are ready. Make sure you have set aside enough time to be able to work through the process. Not only time for writing out all the events and trauma you hold but also time in the forthcoming days perhaps weeks or even months to process and honour any pain or tears you may need to shed.

'Heaven knows we need never be ashamed of our tears, for they are rain upon the blinding dust of earth, overlying our hard hearts. I was better after I had cried, than before - more sorry, more aware of my own ingratitude, more gentle'
- *Charles Dickens*

I recommend having a bath before you start your writing work, perhaps light some incense or candles just to help you feel better in yourself before you begin. Make sure you are in a safe space where you can write, cry and feel any emotions you need to.

It's optional where you opt to start documenting your shadow work, I used my book of shadows yet you might decide to keep this work on seperate pieces of paper . I appreciate many witches couldn't think of anything worse than keeping their list of trauma so do what feels best for you.

I hope that once you have listed all your recollection of traumatic events you start to feel lighter, just like I did. This should be a cathartic experience. Some things to consider to perhaps help you towards starting the process are to look at some of these events as teachers, you have to relive some of these experiences through writing about them in order to heal them but also that you cannot move forward and heal these wounds until you bring them into the light.

Many of us will discover we disassociated from the event that happened to us, downplayed its seriousness, distorted how it was remembered or even changed the story in our head completely in order to make it more palatable. Others may have been present in the event or trauma who told us not to be overdramatic or who told us how we perceived it isn't how it played out perhaps for their own benefit, dark intentions or their own inability to contend what took place.

If you feel traumatised from an event it's still trauma, no one should be able to undermine your feelings if they are affecting you. When you come to write about any individuals involved with your trauma please don't hold back, write down exactly how they made you feel. Don't discount this part of the process, it really validates your pain. If other people were at fault within your trauma you must accept that closure isn't always available to us, we often have to create that closure ourselves. I have someone in my past who truly did me dirty and I struggled with the fact I never believed they could do that to me, but that says more about them than me.

Most of the time people's actions are never about us, completely about them so we must learn to not take it personally. Also accept some people will never and have no ability to apologise, again this says more about them than us but do we still want to be here drinking the poison expecting them to suffer? When is enough enough? If a person attached to your trauma is still in your life we cannot change them, we must recognise that no matter how much you want them to act in a certain way to help provide closure following a traumatic event it can only come from them. It's like waiting for a cat to bark and you will forever end up frustrated and feeling a sense of lack waiting on them to do right by you.

I long held the belief that if this one person in my life could just apologise to me and explain why they did what they did it would have the effect of a magic wand being waved and all my sadness and anger would disappear into thin air. I decided just before one of my birthdays (always a day that triggers thoughts of the past for me) that this wound only ever reopened and triggered my thoughts when I wasn't looking after myself properly or was feeling triggered by something else. Instead of me sitting with my feelings of discomfort, fear or anxiety I would pin them to this fantasy where this individual would show up demonstrating remorse and apologise profusely. I always know when that fantasy starts coming up for me that this is my sneaky shadow convincing me that this person can make everything better when I know it's really my inner child saying "please can you give me some attention, I am struggling with feeling unworthy because of this situation" or "this recent event really triggered this memory and feeling for me, can you just...". Try to see what comes up for you when a specific feeling arises, how does your cunning shadow try to divert you?

Once you have started to love and honour your inner child it's good to start focusing on ways you can reparent them going forward.

The Awakened Witch

ways to reparent your inner child

- Set boundaries within your relationships - understand that this may even cause the relationship to sever
- Reconnect with your body, feelings and emotions
- Reconsider previously held beliefs, thoughts, patterns and behaviours
- Realise that not every thought we have should be believed
- Work on self-love, compassion and forgiveness for our mistakes

- Accept and work on reassuring and reparenting our inner child
- Take on personal accountability
- Avoid drama, conflict, gossip and judgement
- Let go of friends, family members, jobs and anything that is toxic for us
- Prioritise self care and creates time to be alone
- Work on understanding their personal likes, dislikes, needs, goals

Once you finally feel the dark veil of your shadow begin to lift you will hopefully start to feel lighter, more positive and somewhat curious for your future. Shadow work can be an entirely liberating experience and can completely change your core belief systems and also what you want out of your life. For me life was never the same after wading through the dark treacle of shadow work, once I came out on the other side my take on everything changed, far less patience for drama, the shedding of a number of acquaintances, having completely different desires far removed from the normal constraints of society and a loving acceptance of myself. I felt emboldened to make serious and scary decisions to change my life dramatically and finally step into a life I had desired for over a decade and it felt good.

Once you let a lot go it only makes sense for you and the universe to start bringing in the new, the universe abhors a vacuum, but you need to be extremely specific on what you do want. I believe this not only gives you a plan to work on to co-create with the universe but also guidance for any spell or ritual work you may need to carry out.

No matter how big your dreams are, you might find that once you tackle shadow work you have the ability to move forward without so much weighing you down.

The Witches Tool Box

Healing can be an incredibly crooked path between sublime highs and intense lows, it helps to be prepared when you are embarking on this courageous journey. In early recovery from alcohol addiction I built myself my own witches toolbox for times when I was really struggling and would revel in the contents when I really needed it.

A witches toolbox is a great resource to help when you need to shift your mental state. You may have come across these boxes under names such as self-care box or self soothe box, although some of the contents may be fluffy, I have known many addicts to construct one and add it as a major part of their battalion in the bid towards sobriety. These boxes are a strong resource for any form of healing.

In my early days of working on sobriety my tool kit really got me excited over how my new life could be. I started to consider what I could put into this box that would help me to feel soothed, content and would be a healthy go to. I started to visualise the new me that used these tools and could calm and soothe herself.

The task of building up my self soothe box was so delicious because it had me considering what I could go to for a sense of calm and serenity. It distracted my monkey mind and had me curating all the ingredients I needed and constructing my kit. It had me daydreaming over who exactly future me was, this witch who could open this magical box and start to give herself the self-soothing and love she needed.

Self soothe boxes can contain anything you like, you may wish to incorporate a candle, essential oils such as lavender, cinnamon or rose (take the time to figure out what scents soothe your soul), your favourite bubble bath/shower gel or bath bomb, your favourite book that offers comfort. Mine include Women who run with the Wolves by Clarissa Pinkola Estes, Romancing the Ordinary by Sarah Ban Breathnach and Seasons of Moon and Flame by Danielle Dulsky. All three books focus on the wild woman within, the gritty bones of our deepest darkest feelings but also how we are whole, just as we are no matter where we are at. These are some of the most reassuring beautifully written books I possess for darker times such as those when I need to turn to my witches toolbox.

You may wish to add incense sticks (rose incense sticks are my go to for troubled times) perhaps a blanket that was passed down to you from an ancestor or one that just feels cosy and comforting, maybe a warm jumper knitted by a grandma or just one you happened to pick up for yourself, a journal for when you feel compelled to write all that's heavy on your heart but only if this feels like the right thing to do on opening your witches toolbox, after all we are opening this box to feel better. Why not add a sweet treat such as your favourite chocolate bar or candy, maybe some decadent Earl Grey or rose tea, whatever your preference! perhaps a cup and saucer that belonged to your great great grandmother that you only dig out for special occasions such as now. You might wish to add to your box a soothing sensuous body lotion or face mask, perhaps some crystals that you have already cast intentions upon for self-love, my go to crystals for terrible times include a chunk of delicious rose quartz for self-love and my smoky quartz which is a great crystal for addiction.

You may want to create and add to your box a list of things you can do, watch, listen to that you know bring you to a calm place. Perhaps list some films that you can easily access when you need, I recommend keeping it safe on this front. What you don't want to do is add to the list a film or program that has further triggers to set you off, you might have certain pieces of music that you turn to when feeling low and may want to chuck your headphones on and zone out listening to them. Again tread carefully with what you opt to listen to, some of my favourite artists lyrics are very deep and can set me off.

You might want to add a list of important phone numbers to your witches toolbox, if you are battling addiction you might have a sponsor from AA, NA or OA that you can reach out to, perhaps a trusted friend or family member. You may have resources such as a guided meditation, or something you can watch or listen to.

Perhaps you have some cherished letters from family members or friends you can add to your box, my most important letter I ever received was from my grand-mother Rose who lived to 100 years old. She had life figured out, my nan!. She baked and tended her garden to make herself happy, she was also a minimal-ist before it was a thing! My nan was a curator of the simple life and it seemed to work. At a time when I was younger and really struggling with my mental health, nanny Rose wrote me a letter in her cute curly old lady writing. In her letter she explained that whenever she felt a bit out of sorts she would tidy and clean her little home from top to bottom and it always made her feel all was right with the world.

Nanny Rose had a point that I am sure all house witches will stand by. A good cleaning session can completely transform the energy within both you and your environment and is not to be underestimated, it is even shown to help with anxiety and depression. I struggle with overwhelm when I am feeling at my lowest so sometimes I find it's worth setting a timer and just encouraging myself to do an hour's worth of tidying. I often set that timer and before I know it the washing has made my flat smell divine with the scent of lemons, my candles are burning away, the music's going and I am burning up the anxious energy that's been eating me alive. I then find myself tired but hap-pily sitting in a fresh and clean home a few hours later. The message in that letter stays with me all these years on and I regularly start cleaning my home when I am feeling down.

I also think of Amy Winehouse's song 'wake up alone' where she belts out 'got so sick of crying, so just lately, when I catch myself, I do a one-eighty, I stay up, clean the house, at least I'm not drinking. Run around just so I don't have to think about thinking'.

Once again Amy was onto something, although you don't want to numb out your feelings entirely during the healing process a healthy distraction such as cleaning can come in handy. I for one in early stages of sobriety found myself stocking up on lemony cleaning products and powering through house witch books on making floor washes and the like to keep me busy. Not only was I now sober but I had a gleaming household to boot.

Coming back to ingredients for our Witches Tool Kit, once you have packed everything up into your box that you feel you could possibly need you may want to carry out the following ritual.

Healing Initiation Ritual

Tools

- Pink Candle for self-love, nurturing, compassion

- Yellow Candle for happiness, healing for the mind and body, self-confidence and self-esteem (If you don't have coloured candles to hand white candles can be used for anything at all. White is a neutral colour!)

- Any crystals you wish to use throughout your healing process but examine their specific properties to ensure they match to what you need to call on them for. My go to crystals are rose quartz for self-love and inner healing, moonstone for calming any chaotic energy and managing stress, smoky quartz for neutralising negative emotions, removing fear, lifting depression and negative thoughts. It also brings emotional calmness and helps with stress and anxiety.

- Sage bundle or incense (whatever you use to smoke cleanse, abalone shell, salt to extinguish)

- Sheets of plain paper and a pen

- If you work with deities or your ancestor's you may wish to have an offering or libation bowl ready to leave following your work.

As ever I recommend carrying out the goddess mode preparation for this ritual, you will wish to start this ritual clean, fresh and feeling calm. Ensure you have all you need for the ritual and if you cast circles as part of your spell work focus on this first.

If you work with your deities or ancestors I recommend asking them as you cast your circle if they might oversee your work and be by your side for this ritual.

Place your candles in front of you within your circle, as you light your pink candle say the following words -

"I light this candle in honour of the self-love I hold
for myself and I am tending to throughout my
healing journey. I am worthy and deserving of love
and healing and I am stepping into my highest
self and power to move forward along my path. I
hold only good intentions for myself going forward.
So mote it be..."

Feel free to craft your intention statement however resounds most with you, this has to come from your heart.

Now light your yellow candle and say the following words -

"I light this candle in honour of the confidence I
possess, draw upon and build to improve my self-
esteem and self-love. May this candle light the way
for me towards happiness, courage and healing.
So mote it be"

If you work with your deities or ancestors you may wish to call upon them however you see fit, for example I call to Hekate and the Morrigan and put together the following invocation.

"Hekate, Queen of Witchcraft, I ask if you will
help me on my new journey and shine your light in
your role as torch bearer for me to see my way
forward on my healing journey. Guide me from
this liminal space or crossroads I find myself in

now between my current circumstances and the
new life I wish to step into"

"Morrigan, Great Queen, I ask if you will help me
forward on my new path and help me invoke the
courage and strength akin to yours to transform
my life and to be victorious in taking action and
confronting my fears to move forward"

After calling upon your deities or ancestors take a few moments in silence, perhaps meditation to listen to any messages or guidance you may receive. Once you feel inspired take your pen and paper. You want to begin to channel the energy you have raised and hopefully your deities too! Write yourself a letter addressing it to yourself and begin to outline only the good you see within you, now this might be tricky if you are struggling on the self-worth front but dig deep.

Consider things you are good at, what you like about your personality, achievements that you are proud of, compliments you have received that you adore. Address your letter as if you are actually writing to yourself. This letter is important and you need to consider that the words imparted are those you will wish to hear in your darkest of times so ensure you are as loving, kind and compassionate as you can be. You want this letter to make you feel seen, loved and cared for. You might want to reassure future you that you won't give up on your healing journey, you know it feels tough right now or that in this moment you might feel you have gone backwards but this is part of the process - you are so strong and you can do this.

Once you feel you have added everything you wish to impart in your letter, fold it up and put it to one side ready to put into your witches toolbox following this ritual.

You now want to take your crystal or crystals as we are going to lay an intention on them. These can provide a comfort blanket throughout your healing process.

Start by smoke cleansing your crystals, whatever your preference, light your smoke cleansing tool and direct the smoke across the entirety of your crystal. If you use sage, holding an abalone shell with salt in to extinguish when you are finished and a feather to direct the smoke is really helpful for any smoke cleansing you carry out in your practice. Once you feel your crystals are fully cleansed and you have extinguished your smoke cleansing tool, take your first crystal. You can use one or as many crystals as you choose for this, I settled on using two.

Sit with your crystal in your dominant magick hand, you may wish to meditate upon your crystal or focus your gaze upon it. Now decide the gift this crystal is going to bring to you going forward in your healing process, will it be serenity? reassurance when things get tough?

Don't overthink it too much but just consider a couple of words of how this crystal will help or make you feel.

To cast that intention upon your crystal you might opt to say a few words over it for example, "rose quartz, I ask that you hold for me self-love and compassion" or "moonstone, I ask that you bring me calming energy in chaotic times". Based upon the properties of your specific crystals, adjust this accordingly. If you don't feel connected to your crystal for this intention immediately don't panic, you will be building a relationship with your crystal following this ritual which I will come to shortly.

Once you have worked your way through your crystals giving each an intention, begin to start closing your circle. Thank your deities or ancestors for spending this time with you and for their help going forward. Ensure you leave any offerings or a libation bowl upon your altar for them.

You can now add your carefully crafted letter of love to yourself to your witches toolbox for when your future self truly needs it.

In respect of your crystals I recommend you keep these on you at all times throughout your healing journey, keep them in your bra, your handbag, in your pocket, wallet, place them at the side of your bath or shower when you bathe. Most importantly sleep with them under your pillow or next to you in bed each night. Hold them when you feel disempowered, when you feel fired up or have achieved something along your journey. I cannot tell you how reassuring I have found it to have my crystals to hand especially if I am out and about and something knocks me off course, it reconnects me to my pledge to my healing process and solidifies for me that there are good and bad days along the way but that I have made the promise to myself to work on my healing process come what may. Through this I can also connect with my deities who were present with me in that magickal moment of calling upon their guidance and support.

The Moon

My obsession with the moon started as a toddler following obsessively watching the children's program Button Moon. I would constantly ask my dad if we could go down to the bottom of the garden and say goodnight to Button Moon, who in the program was the star of the show.

In later years my dad became increasingly aware of how much my behaviour was affected by the full moon. When chaos ensued with me he said he often would take a look up at the sky at night and could guarantee the moon would be full.

He never let me in on this until my adult years, it was just a hunch he had. I had no awareness in my younger years just how much power the moon had over nature, humans and animals. Although it has never been successfully scientifically proven I wholeheartedly stand by the moon's supposed effects on us mere mortals, after all our bodies are up to 75% water and the moon has the ability to affect the tides. There has to be something within that.

I regularly start my period on a new moon, this is classed a white moon cycle which is a common time for most women's monthlies to commence. Red moon cycle is the term for commencing your period on a full moon, historically many of the women who started over the full moon period were seen as healers or medicine women as they were able to provide care to menstruating women who were generally experiencing their cycle over the new moon. It's more common for women to ovulate over a full moon and have their period over a new moon.

Childbirth rates are said to be at a high on a full moon, I gave birth to my own daughter under a full moon in July 2007, the same year that in the UK, several police forces throughout the country ramped up the amount of police officers they put to work on full moon nights in a bid to deal with increased criminal activity. Deaths of the elderly are also said to peak on a new or full moon.

Hippocrates believed that no physician should be able to treat disease without a knowledge of astronomy and Aristotle discussed the effect within his works on the human body, he believed with the brain being the most moist organ of the body this could explain the moon's effect upon our mental state akin to its effect on the tides.

Even Shakespeare acknowledged the moons ability to affect our sanity within his play Othello

> *"It is the very error of the moon.*
> *She comes more near the earth that she was wont.*
> *And makes men mad"*

If you are new to the craft or working on transforming your life I cannot recommend a better way to start within your practice than to honour and understand the moon's phases. Also to consider the different astrological signs that sit within each full or new moon phase and how this impacts on your life at this time.

New moons and full moons both hold different celestial powers, new moons are all about our intentions so new beginnings and full moons are about affirmations - letting go and completion. By starting our work at the new moon phase we can follow the moon's natural cycle. By setting out intentions we wish to work to at this point we can reach the full moon and consider what we need to let go of, what might be holding us back from achieving the intentions we have set, whereby hopefully we can reach the next new moon having met our intentions.

One of the most important books I highly recommend that has broken down the entire process of honouring that beautiful space egg in the sky is 'Lunar Living – Working with the Magic of the Moon Cycles' written by Kirsty Gallagher. This detailed book has strengthened my understanding and ability to work with the moon through every single phase and zodiac sign; however I hope the following might help you get started.

New Moon

For me working with the new moon can be a tricky time as I am usually awash with the wonderful neurotic feelings that coincides with my monthly cycle. However once I get going I find the days following a new moon I am fired up with new intentions ready for fresh new beginnings.

Firstly give yourself a break if you are feeling particularly tired in and around this phase. New and full moons can affect our sleep either through a longer duration to drift off, shorter sleep periods or experiencing less of a deep sleep.

I like to plan in advance, perhaps a night or two before a new moon what I want to focus my intentions on. If you have trouble tracking the moon it's pretty easy to find a good app or pretty lunar calendar that you can print off to help you monitor all of the phases. I also recommend ascertaining what zodiac sign the new moon will be sitting in, for example the last new moon that passed for me before writing this was in Libra. Before I had determined this I was already tackling issues around balance and committing to a decision, however once I understood the areas of my life that could be affected under this new moon in Libra I felt better equipped to analyse, assess and make changes to those areas.

New moons overall are great times to focus on starting over so working with a clean slate and planting seeds relating to your dreams, projects and starting the creating and manifesting process. The eve before a new moon I will take some time to journal in my book of shadows my new intentions and reflections following on from the last full moon.

New moons are my favourite overall as I love the creation process with my intentions, it's the execution I really need to apply maximum effort to.

On the night of the new moon I like to set aside time for a ritual. If you have a lot of time you can assign you might wish to start by cleaning your home from top to bottom. You might wish to smoke cleanse your home throughout. If using sage, don't forget this acts as a spiritual bleach removing both good and bad energies so you might wish to follow up with burning some juniper in your cauldron or a heat resistant bowl along with a charcoal disk. Juniper is perfect for attracting abundance and prosperity, it is great for purification ahead of a ritual and also awakens the mind and body.

If you haven't time to cleanse your home perhaps just give your altar some tlc. I like to clear up any incense and smoke cleansing ashes, dust and wipe down the surface of my altar, removing any offerings I may have made recently as a moon ritual for me will culminate in me providing new ones. I use my altar daily so I feel it's a mark of respect to my deities before any spell work or rituals I carry out that might require their presence.

I then run myself a bath and indulge in full goddess mode preparations for the night. I gather all the tools together that I will need for my ritual. I would recommend oracle and/or tarot cards, your book of shadows, loose paper, a pen, your cauldron or a bowl of water, matches or a lighter.

I cast my circle as I would normally to signify the beginning of a ritual or my spell work, if you work with deities you may wish to call upon them to help oversee your work.

Once your circle is cast, take the loose paper and your pen or pencil, consider and write down your intentions for the next month. Consider new challenges and goals you would like to set for yourself, really honour your heart's deepest desires.

I mentioned you will need a bowl of water and matches or a lighter as we are going to safely light each strip of paper with our intentions on one at a time in order to send this message out to the moon. Read aloud each intention before you light each piece of paper, consider the intention on the paper as you watch it burn before placing the remaining paper and embers into the water. I have often carried out this ritual on my own or with friends and my daughter outside in my garden at night, this way I have safely been able to burn my pieces of paper but also had the opportunity to stargaze and feel the connection to the moon and night sky as I do. The new moon at this stage is a dark moon, it's the beginning of the moon's rotation and a time when the moon will be facing the earth and in complete darkness.

If you work with your deities or ancestors you might wish to say a few words to ask if they will assist you with your intentions. Once you have finished putting out your intentions to the moon you might wish to pull the following tarot spread to receive any messages in relation to your new intentions.

New Moon Tarot Spread

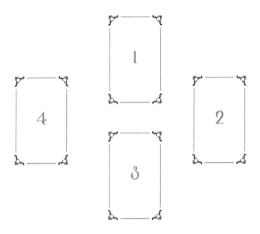

1. What do I need to focus on or take inspired action on in relation to my goals?

2. What blocks do I need to be aware of in relation to my goals?

3. How can I heal or work on these blocks to move forward?

4. What can I expect to manifest following on from this moon cycle and my plan?

I recommend noting any cards and messages you pick up through this reading and adding this to your book of shadows. It's great to look back at each new and full moon to see how your intentions played out.

Once you are finished with your divination and ritual, thank your deities or ancestors for their presence if you did call them in and explain you are finishing up your work. Close down your circle applying the same level of energy used to open. You might wish to take a few moments to ground yourself and settle your energy following this ritual and maybe eat a small snack or replenish your energy through relaxing. Rituals and spell work can really take a lot of energy so it's good to level out following.

Full Moon

My work around a full moon focuses on that which I wish to eliminate from my life so I focus on habits I wish to kill, relationships I need to sever and release from my life, endings to situations that are less than desirable, diminishing a poor mindset I may be holding regarding an area of my life and better managing my negative emotions in order to move forward. It's a time when I consider how far I may have progressed with the seeds I may have planted at the last new moon.

Full moons are more of a reflective period for me to consider what I have or haven't achieved since the new moon, a halfway point to assess how your intentions are coming along. I like to look over the notes I made in my book of shadows at the last new moon and see if I am on track with my actions, if there are any stumbling blocks I have met or if I am already at a point where I can celebrate any wins I might have already had.

Gratitude is key at this point in the moon's cycle, make sure you relish in any success you have had as a result of your new moon plans. If you work with any deities or ancestors be sure to thank them for their assistance. It's worth writing a detailed gratitude list at this point to commemorate all the abundance and joy within your life but to also acknowledge any external factors or people that have had a part to play in your success.

If you haven't moved forward on your dreams don't be too hard on yourself, the full moon can naturally be a highly emotional period for us all without beating yourself up too. This is a great time to assess that dream you originally held, is it still one you covet? What might you do differently or adjust in your plan for this next half of the moon cycle before the next new moon?. I often like to give myself a couple of days reprieve after a full moon before jumping back into action on my goals as I am very conscious of how this moon phase can lead to feelings of frustration, self-doubt and at times even anger!

The following journalling points might offer up reflection for where you find yourself currently with intentions you set upon the new moon -

- What do I need to surrender to currently?
- What does my soul need?

- Which energetic ties do I need to release to move me forward to my dreams?
- What have I been neglecting?
- Where in my life am I out of alignment?
- What beliefs do I need to release?
- What fears do I need to release?
- Where in life have I been playing small?

Moon Water

The new and full moon both give me the opportunity to make moon water, this is a simple process of taking a jug, bottle or jar, smoke cleansing it and then adding fresh clean drinking water to it. I like to state my specific intentions over my moon water, I will document in my book of shadows the intentions I will be using it for and I also create a small tag that I tie with string to my mason jar that outlines the specific full or new moon the water was blessed by, the date and also the type of moon, for example it could be the moon in a particular astrological sign or the name of the full moon relating to the time of year (for example a pink moon, worm moon etc.).

Full moon water is said to hold so much power and can be used for empowering spells, in particular completion spells or spells relating to guidance, decision making or healing and charging items such as crystals or altar tools. You can also make waning moon water which can help with releasing, reflecting and removing things from your life, it's a good moon water to use to rid addictions, bad habits or illness. Waxing moon water is ideal to assist you with planning, creating, courage, luck, motivation, inspiration, manifesting and also growing seeds and plants.

As part of your intentions you may wish to say out loud whilst preparing your moon water

> *"Creating and using this moon water,*
> *I wish to release.........*
> *I use the lunar energy to invite abundance*
> *into my ...."*

Your intention can be double edged and my full and new moon rituals incorporate letting go of specific habits, relationships, situations and calling in the new in all the same areas.

Once I have my jar, bottle or jug of water I wait until night has drawn in and leave it in my garden where the moon can successfully shine its light over it. I don't panic too much if the moon isn't directly over my water, overall my aim is to draw down the moon's energy into the jar. I leave my moon water out all night which can be tricky in the summer as you need to retrieve it before sunrise, it involves me setting an alarm for the early hours to collect it. Alongside my moon water I also like to leave my crystals out to be bathed in the moon's rays.

Moon water has many uses, I have added it to my chalice, added it to recipes I have made, coffee I have brewed, used it to water my plants, added it to my chalice and when casting my circle or for any ritual or spell work when water is the required element, added it to my bath water, floor washes and combined it with essential oil to make cleansing sprays.

Selene

Selene, Isis, Hekate, Diane and Artemis are all lunar deities, however Selene is often said to be the image of the moon itself not just a deity who rules over it. Her Roman name is Lunar and she was said to be able to create lunacy with purpose in mere mortals as and when she chose.

Goddess of the moon from the Greek pantheon, Selene was the daughter of the Titans Hyperion and Theia, with siblings Eos (God of the Dawn) and Helios (Sun God).

Hyperion, her father was said to be the god of heavenly light, his mother was Gaia (Earth) and his father Uranus (Sky). Her mother Theia represented the shining blue colour of the sky and was said to be the Titaness of sight.

Selene is a great deity to work with for lunar magick, healing, intuition, psychic abilities, dreams, emotions but also to become more intimate with our own bodies especially when it comes to female menstrual cycles which are linked to the phases of the moon. Selene is said to be the goddess of childbirth and would make childbirth at night easier than throughout the day. Selene can help us to listen to and develop our intuition and messages from our subconscious but also encourages us to analyse our dreams to seek clarity and perspective.

She is said to ride a silver chariot into the night sky when the moon rises, her chariot is often depicted as being pulled by either two white horses, oxens or bulls but they are always shown as pure white.

Selene wears a gleaming silver crown matching her chariot, her long black hair matching the dark sky in sharp contrast to her pale skin that shines with her own inner light. Each night Selene is said to emerge from the sea upon her chariot however on nights she cannot be seen she does have a good reason for being absent.

Selene took many lovers including Pan and Zeus however her true love was Endymion, a mere mortal who was, depending on which story told, said to be perhaps an astrologer, a simple shepherd, the mortal son of Zeus or even a prince in exile.

Selene was enchanted by him one night as she came across him sleeping under the stars. She came down from the sky to get a better look at him whilst he slept and continued to do this every night, subsequently leaving her chariot behind and the sky pitch black with her absence. It reached a point where she asked her brother Helios the sun god to help out by covering for her nightly shift. A fine plan until Zeus noticed the sky wasn't its usual brightness and that during the day the sun was somewhat lacking.

Zeus finally got to the bottom of what was going on and knew if he didn't intervene chaos would ensue. It's said that Selene asked Zeus to save Endymion from the fate of mere mortals - aging. Zeus agreed and put Endymion into an enchanted sleep in a cave upon Mount Latmus that was marked by moonstones and pure white rocks and watched over by nymphs, this enabled Selene to be able to see Endymion whenever she so chose, taking away the urgency of Selene feeling the need to visit Endymion every night due to time and his mortality, but also meant she wouldn't need to be absent during the night therefore she couldn't affect the celestial skies as before. Other lore states that Zeus put Endymion to sleep as a form of punishment and that due to his sympathy for Selene he didn't kill him outright. Another telling is that Endymion asked to enter an ageless sleep over a mortal life in a bid to never be parted from Selene. Selene was said to visit Endymion within his dreams and make love to him; she birthed fifty daughters by him as a result.

Working with Selene you might wish to add to your altar or sacred space depictions of the moon, white horses, silver jewellery or charms, moon water and selenite crystals.

> *'Pray to the moon when she is round*
> *Luck with you shall then abound*
> *What you seek for shall be found*
> *In sea or sky or solid ground'*

Heartbroken Witch

Heartbreak as a witch has always been an area I have struggled with, hasn't everyone?. Romantic relationships are a big work in progress for me, as a witch I have found it incredibly disempowering to grieve and heal from a lost love as in some sense for that period of time it has felt as though the source of my power has been taken away. I now measure my grief and heartbreak in relation to how much love I am able to give out and for that I am truly proud. It's better to have loved and lost rather than never to have loved at all, or as my very good friend Alex says 'It is better to have loved and lost than to be stuck with the psycho for the rest of your life'. I wonder if you can relate to her sentiments?

Failed relationships can be incredibly difficult to recover from, any long term partner I have had has always been a best friend too so their loss has been immense. Grieving for someone who's still alive is strange, let alone having to deal with each other moving on to find new partners or even co-parenting. We underestimate how difficult a process this can be, at times it can also feel that you and your ex might be pitched against one another to see who heals the fastest, has a glow up, moves on to someone else first. I constantly have to remind myself the process of grieving needs to take as long as it needs.

When I came to writing this book I was absolutely heartbroken and the separation really haunted me. It took me around a year and a half to fully get to a place of acceptance and understanding following our breakup. I believe the connection with my last partner was karmic, we were meant to be within each other's lives for that period of time and to teach one another a lesson so we could grow for the next stage within our existence.

I felt a lot of shame and embarrassment for holding such intense feelings of sadness and grief for this person for so long but I also accept this is a reflection for how deeply and truly I love. These feelings came in waves and I would think I had really moved through a lot of grief and pain and that was no longer taking up as much space within my mind to other days when I would dream about him or a memory would arise and I would find myself back in the process again.

I recognise how healthy it is to work through these emotions when they come up, allow yourself as much time as you need. In the same breath I was also conscious of not allowing myself to wallow and if I found myself doing that I would often recognise I was lacking in the self love department.

Before you embark on spell work can I recommend writing a letter to your ex that you never post? just to get everything out that needs to be said. Everything……. Don't hold back, you might opt to do this as part of a full moon ritual and burn it to send it out into the ether.

I also recommend smoke cleansing your environment to remove their energy, ensuring you spend more time cleansing areas that you spent more time together, perhaps a dining table, sofa, bed or even your car. Leave a window open in each room you smoke cleanse to allow any negative energy relating to that relationship to leave and perhaps utter some words from the heart as you go along asking to remove your ex's energy from your space.

In terms of the spell work and rituals within this book I have given you the specific work I carried out myself relating to breakups, protection and self-love that were very necessary within my own healing process.

Healing Heart Spell

This is a spell I came across from The Traveling Witch website, a wonderful resource. This is one of the most powerful symbolic spells I have come across following my own heartbreak.

Tools
  A beetroot
  Paper
  A Pen or pencil
  Knife or carving tool

The beetroot is symbolic of your poor broken heart, before we start the spell make sure you have cleaned up the beetroot and removed the green shoots. You might opt to carry out this spell outside as it can get a bit messy, alternatively lay a towel out if you are doing this inside.

Cast your circle or carry out any of your usual formalities before your spell work. Take the beetroot and your knife. Draw on all your heartbreak, grief and raw emotion and apply it to the beetroot. Start to cut, stab, carve into it in a way that feels cathartic. Cry over it, scream, shout at it, pour out all your heartache all over it.

Once you are done and you feel all that emotion has washed over you take your paper and write out your intentions.

Create some words from the heart, for example –

> *'My heart is healing, allow this pain and hurt to pass and my heart to come back to life despite all the suffering it has experienced.*
> *I am open to self-love and love from others.*
> *So mote it be'*

Tailor your words however you see fit but in a way that resounds with you.

Cut a hole into the centre of your beetroot (symbolic of your heart), roll your intentions paper into a small scroll and insert it into the hole of your beetroot. Take your beetroot and bury it into the ground, as it decomposes the earth reclaims it allowing your heartbreak and grief to leave.

Banishing Spell Jar

This is a great spell to remove someone from your life fully to enable you to move on, make sure you are prepared for them to be fully removed from your life!

Tools

Vinegar – *sours and dissolves relationships*
Ground or fresh ginger – *speeds up spells*
Black pepper – *used to banish negativity and for courage*
Garlic clove– *used to repel negativity and for courage and strength*
Onion skin – *used to banish, protects you against your enemies*
Paper
Pen or pencil
Jam jar or small glass jar
Black candle
Lighter or matches

Fill your glass jar around two thirds full of vinegar, grate fresh ginger or sprinkle ground ginger into your jar, then sprinkle black pepper or add black peppercorns, a clove of garlic and onion skin.

Write on a small piece of paper the full name of who you wish to remove from your life. Fold the paper up as small as you can and drop it into the jam jar. Put the lid on your jar. Take your small black candle and light it, allow the wax to drop over the lid of your jar and to effectively seal in your spell. Take care as you carry out this part not to get hot wax over you.

Once the wax has cooled take your jar in your hands and shake it – create your own chant or use the following below –

> '(name of who you are removing) I release you
> and I believe, it's for the best for you and me. So
> mote it be'

Traditionally for a banishing spell jar it's recommended you bury the spell jar far from your home or leave it on a crossroads however this might prove tricky and impractical for some - I have simply taken the spell jar with me on a long walk and thrown it in a bin!

Cut the Cord Ritual

Tools
> Tarot Cards *or a photograph of you and one of who you are cutting cords with*
> A piece of string
> Scissors

This spell is also inspired by The Traveling Witch website, Avery who runs the site was my go to at the time of carrying out spells pertaining to my heartbreak.

I carried out this ritual using two tarot cards to represent me and my ex love. I used two tarot cards to represent me and my ex-partner (the Empress and the Magician), alternatively you can use a photo of you and one of your ex.

You must be ready to fully cut all ties with your ex partner, sit in your circle with the photograph or tarot card representing you on your left hand side and your ex's photograph or representative tarot card to the right. Lay the string out between the opposing photos or tarot cards.

Touch the string that connects the two photographs or tarot cards, close your eyes and visualise being within a white room with your ex partner standing in front of you. Spend time in this room with your ex – you might need to cry, kiss, shout, scream, hug. See what comes up.

This might even indicate you aren't ready to fully let go yet too, if that does become apparent to you don't panic but do shut down your spell work and come back to it as and when you feel the time is right.

This space gives you the opportunity to say or do anything you feel the need to with your ex, remember to keep your original intentions in mind whilst you are here. Once you feel you have exhausted the interaction with your ex and it feels done say goodbye to them and slowly open your eyes.

Take your scissors and cut through the string to complete your spell.

Post Breakup Spell Jar for Healing and Self-Love

This is the perfect spell jar to create following on from a breakup to help get you on the road to recovery.

Tools

Rose petals – *for self-love and to open the heart*
Pink salt – *banishes sadness, cleanses doubt and renews self-love*
Sugar – *for self-attraction*
Moon water – *to empower your spell*
Cinnamon – *for personal power*
Olive oil – *to promote healing*
Rose quartz crystal – *to increase self-worth, self-esteem, assist forgiveness, open your heart*
Thyme – *for courage and strength*
Personal item to you – *perhaps a photograph of you, cutting of your hair or simply write your name on a piece of paper*
Jam jar
Pink candle
Matches or lighter

Feel free to use as much or as little as you feel is needed for each ingredient – adjust the volumes of the ingredients in accordance to what you feel you need to bring more of into your life. Swap out certain ingredients if you feel necessary, the main thing we want to bring to our spell work is our intention. Combine all the ingredients in your jar and once ready add your personal item.

Place the lid on the jar securely, light your pink candle and allow the wax to safely drip across and around the jar's seal. Once the wax has cooled and sealed recite the following chant or create your own –

'I return all love back to me, three times three,
so mote it be'

Chant and raise the energy up around you. Keep this spell jar on your altar, you might wish to carry it with you (providing it is sealed correctly) and give it a good shake and repeat the chant on the daily.

Ancestral Magic

'Let the story of who you were send shivers down
the spines of our granddaughters. Let them hear
about you as the woman who was herself who did
her own thing and helped others along the way'
-Tanya Markul

I was working on my grimoire around Samhain and it
made me consider how important it is for me to pass
this down to my daughter Amelie should she decide to
follow the same crooked path. My grimoire feels very
sacred to me, it's not perfect by any means, I am far
from artistic therefore my grimoire relies heavily on
printed pictures, pressed flowers and photographs for
the visuals.

Ancestral magick had started to become a key theme
for me around this time too with Samhain fast
approaching, it also coincided with my dad discovering one of his old unprocessed camera films from the
eighties. He processed it in his dark room not knowing

what was on it only for pictures of me, my brother and our deceased grandparents to materialise.

I decided to honour my immediate ancestors at my altar by adding their photographs to my altar. I played Louis Armstrong music in homage to my grandad Denis (his name was always spelt with one n!) who loved to listen to him and jazz overall whilst he swished whisky around in a tumbler in the grand front room of his home in Bodmin, Cornwall. That Samhain I burnt multiple candles and incense at my altar, me and my daughter cast a circle together and carried out some spell work in relation to what we wished to release for that night and what we wished to bring in, asking our ancestors for their assistance.

The veil is thin throughout Samhain and the darker seasons so it can be the perfect time to start working on ancestral magick. You may feel this has more relevance to you than perhaps working with a deity, after all who better to work with than those we have the same DNA running through our veins? Working with our ancestors may feel more real and powerful than working with deities, these ancestors walked on this very plain and through being linked to us by blood they may have more interest in your success as an ascendant of them.

The ancestral work I have carried out since that Samhain has involved immediate ancestors that I had known, however you can call upon ancestors throughout centuries of your lineage to assist you with your magick work and offer you guidance and protection and their wisdom.

Many of us have stories that run throughout our family, particular characters within our bloodline that stand out that you may wish to call upon. I have a particular ancestor who lived a fairly straightforward mundane life until a Swedish sea captain arrived at the local port and charmed her. Within three days she had decided to run away to sea with him for some real adventures leaving behind her safe, normal life here in the UK. I have always had a fondness for that relative, her wild desire for the new and no fear in obtaining it.

I have another ancestor by family marriage called John Benge, said to be a wife beating alcoholic who worked on the train tracks of south London. His drunkenness and poor attention at work was the cause of a horrendous train accident on the Folkestone to London train that killed many in the Victorian era. Charles Dickens happened to be one of the passengers on that train, one of mine amongst many others favourite authors. The injuries Dickens sustained within that train crash were the cause of his death many years later – many of us have ancestors we wouldn't want to touch with a barge pole and you may wish to be specific on who you are calling in if you feel a certain ancestors presence is not required. If karma is anything to go by, a few years later John Benge decided to take a shortcut through a train tunnel in Penge, south London late at night following a heavy drinking session at the local pub. He was hit by a train whilst walking through the tunnel and died on impact, to this day sightings of his ghost are frequently reported and have been documented in literature.

You might feel the need to carry out some ancestral healing within your own practice, I truly believe the theory that by healing ourselves we heal a further seven generations within our line. There may be certain behaviours or health issues that run throughout your family tree and through trying to understand our relatives and their issues we can sometimes have more compassion and understanding of our own. Having had my own issues with alcohol I can in some respects understand my ancestor John Benge's plight when it came to alcohol dependency and his subsequent actions and offer some compassion however I struggle to understand how someone could hurt so many through their behaviour and negligence.

It's certainly worth asking older generations of relatives that you have, what light they can shed on these stories, it also keeps the old stories alive for you to pass onto your own future generations. You might even hear about long forgotten family traditions that you wish to restart out of respect and homage to them, or even opt to start some of your own and document them within your grimoire for future generations to discover.

You may find that you haven't any relatives that particularly resonate with you. It is possible to look further into your cultural heritage through ancestry companies online that offer DNA tests that can trace exactly where your bloodline originated from. I looked at my parents genealogy to discover we are mainly of Celtic origin hailing from Ireland, Scotland, Cornwall, and a few other parts of the UK but also Sweden and Brittany, France. This inspired me to start to look into the old traditional stories that linked to the Celts which ultimately tapped further into the magic of those tribes. My particular interest within my heritage links to the hedge witches, healers and folk magick.

Ancestral magick can be a sensitive part of the craft for some, my grandad Denis was adopted and shunned by his birth family when he did locate them and tried to reach out to them in his fifties. Adoption can make looking into immediate ancestors troubling however you may still feel the call to work with your ancestors, perhaps decide to understand or find out more about your cultural background and connect to your ancestors even if you don't have a physical connection to your birth family. You do not need to know the names of your ancestors or even who they were in order to honour and work with them. Alternatively if you feel more connected to your adoptive family there's absolutely nothing stopping you from working with whoever feels like family to you.

If you do know the name of an ancestor and wish to call them into your practice you might wish to say their name three times to open the lines of communication. In the same manner as you might work with a deity for your spell or ritual work you can ask your ancestors to be present with you as you open your circle and ask them to help oversee and support the work you are there to carry out. Let them know politely when you are finishing up. Again, I would never recommend dismissing a deity or ancestor when your work is complete to avoid appearing outrageously disrespectful, kindly let them know your work is finished up and thank them for their support and protection. In the same principle as working with deities I recommend leaving an offering to thank them for their support. This can be a wonderful way to show gratitude especially if you know what that ancestor was particularly privy to as you can tailor your offerings accordingly.

You might wish to add your offerings to your altar or even create an ancestral altar. If you hold photographs of any ancestors you are working with you may wish to have these as a mainstay on your altar, you might opt to leave out a fresh glass or chalice of water and burn incense or candles daily to demonstrate your gratitude, for special occasions such as anniversaries or birthdays relevant to them or your family, if you honour the sabbaths you might offer up special items to them on these special days. Be it their favourite aftershave or perfume, tobacco, flowers or plants they loved, heirlooms they may have passed down to you, letters or cards received from them, their favourite tipple or food. You could even play music you know they enjoyed. If you are working with ancestors from centuries back you may wish to use traditional music that links to your heritage.

You might wish to carry out daily devotion with your ancestors, similar to how I outlined with deities through spending time daily in meditation, prayer and communication with your ancestors. I often call on my nanny Rose when I am in dire straits or simply to notify her of what's happening within my life. I know she might be open to these conversations as I recall her explaining how she always wished my grandad good morning and how she would let him know what was happening in her life following his passing many years before. She believed he was on the other side of the veil listening so I believe she would be open to having the same conversations with me.

You may want to seek out messages from your ancestors through divination using tarot or oracle cards through stating any questions you may have either out loud or in your mind and see what comes up. You may also wish to see if you connect with an ancestor through your dreams. Before you go to sleep ask a particular ancestor if they will come to you within your dreams, if you have a particular issue you would like their guidance with ask them if they might help you or offer you guidance once you connect within your dream. It's worth noting any messages you might receive in your book of shadows or journal. This is a new endeavour for me and I haven't had my nanny Rose come through yet however on my last attempt to meet with her I dreamt I was in her former kitchen where we baked together when I was a child.

Once you strengthen the lines of connection with your ancestors you may find you receive direct messages or your psychic abilities increase significantly. It's wise to build up a practice of continuous demonstration of devotion and respect, same as you would with a deity, rather than just coming to them whenever you want something.

Ancestor Tarot Spread

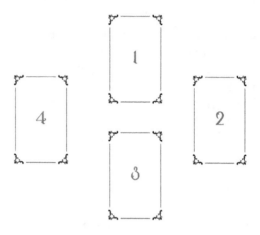

1. Who are the ancestors joining you in this reading?

2. A message from your ancestors

3. How has your past been affected by family trauma?

4. What do your ancestors want you to know about your future?

The Wild Remedy

'I understood at a very early age that in nature I felt everything I should feel in church but never did. Walking in the woods, I felt in touch with the universe and with the spirit of the universe'
-Alice Walker

Nature to me has always been the witch's form of church. I am never happier than when the sun is shining and I am out tending my garden growing seeds or carrying out general garden husbandry whilst listening to the birds sing.

I also built on my love of the land by looking into my ancestral roots. I discovered my heritage was pretty much British, Scottish and Irish and this sparked a real interest in looking at how ancestors of mine might have lived on, honoured and worked the land.

I gobbled up information in regards to folk magick especially from Scotland where I feel strongly connected to and I have Scottish lineage on my dad's side of the family up to my great grandfather. I delved into saining, animism, native plants and how they were used within magick and medicine, some of which we will look at within the medicine woman chapter of this book.

Researching my heritage made me feel part of a bigger picture within the world. I realised we all come from generations of individuals whose choices and fate have led us to where we are today. This inspired me to immerse myself in reading many stories and myths linked to my native lands.

> *'Stories are medicine. I have been taken with stories since I heard my first. They have such power; they do not require that we do, be, act anything - we need only listen. The remedies for repair or reclamation of any lost psychic drive are contained in stories. Stories engender the excitement, sadness, questions, longings and understandings that spontaneously bring the archetype, in this case Wild Woman, back to the surface'*
>
> *- Women who run with the Wolves - Clarissa Pinkola-Estes*

I urge you to look into stories within your own heritage, I am sure you will find medicine within them. Beginning to research the various deities, you might find you begin to have a love for their individual stories and interest perhaps within a particular pantheon linked to your own ancestry. This may strengthen your connection to the land you live on as you may identify particular places of interest close to where you live that have stories linked to your culture or ancestors.

I found that once I understood more about how my ancestors lived, the sabbaths became more important to me. I understood how integral each harvest was, how the land could hold you to such mercy but through honouring each harvest I could really witness the changes that occurred throughout the year, connect to the land and keep alive the honour of each sabbath. This also became my responsibility to keep alive and pass down these traditions to my daughter for future ancestors. I also benefit from enjoying and sharing the festivities with my family and friends.

The sabbaths and understanding of the farming year enabled me to understand how much the earth and sun can provide to us. With the passing of each sabbath I had a time marker to compare how much the land had changed since the last. I document many of the sabbaths through taking photographs of breads or cakes I made (sabbaths are amazing if you love cake and dough like me ha!), celebrations I hosted such as picnics, dinners, days out, historical information regarding each sabbath and traditional celebrations and the lore linked to them.

I discovered how thin the veil is on Beltane one year when wandering across a field in the middle of the night with my ex partner. We were laughing and joking whilst returning from walking a friend home. Suddenly we heard a demonic growl come from a corner of the woods. We rushed home and spent most the night thereafter feeling something had followed

143

and was watching us. Beltane is when the veil between the human world and spirit world is thin - whatever was in that field didn't want us there!

During my research regarding Samhain and Beltane I discovered that saining rituals were carried out within Scottish folk magick at these two sabbaths. Saining is the Scots word for blessing, protecting and consecrating. Saining was used to remove unwanted spirits from people, cattle and the land.

At the sabbath festivals communities would gather and hold saining ceremonies. Sacred fires such as the one at the Nede fire would be used to light the fires used at these festivals, people would jump over the flames or walk in between them in a bid to be sained. The community would also light their own hearth fires from this sacred fire.

New born babies would be sained through the use of pine candles, mothers and midwives would speak charms and walk deosil (clockwise) around the newborn baby's bed.

Pine candles give off a black smoke, they are resinous and aromatic and come from the stump of the pine trees when they fall down. It can burn for a long time so would have been used to light fires or as a form of candle.

Cattle would be sained if they were believed to be elf-shot, ancient medical texts document cattle being shot at by fairies or elves with invisible arrows - stone arrowheads they used were referred to as either fairy darts, elf arrows or elfshot. This sounds far-fetched yet laws still stand within Icelandic environmental impact assessment process when they are breaking ground on the land to protect elven habitat.

Doctors were rarely able to isolate and demonstrate an elf shot wound and this was put down to the elves being such a good shot. Healers turned to magick and religion to treat elfshot, a mixture of psychology, sympathetic magick, prayers and plant concoctions drawing upon each plant's properties.

A collection of nine powerful herbs were collated by the Anglo-Saxons, these plants were mugwort, plantain, lambs cress, nettle, betony, chamomile, crab-Apple, thyme and fennel. These herbs were often harvested at Litha when they were said to hold the most magickal and medicinal power. They would be used throughout the year for medicine but also burnt upon the Litha celebratory fires.

The nine herbs would be boiled and added to old soap and apple residue to form a paste, the nine herbs charm would be sung by healers three times over each herb as it was being prepared, then into the injured individuals mouth, ears and over their wounds before it would be applied as a salve. These rituals used the power of numbers, the number three and nine were viewed as magickal numbers within themselves, three is said to be the number of perfection and the number nine (made up of three times three) was regarded as the number of completion. The nine herbs charm details the nine herbs and their properties but also references the god Odin (Woden), the Germanic god of wisdom and knowledge. Healers used rituals that included charms, songs and rhymes that provided entertainment but also set the stage for healing to take place. Ancient healers were already aware of the placebo effect before we had psychological proof to back it up, they recognised the mind and body connection and how an individual's belief that a cure being successful will give it a greater chance of working.

> *'These nine have power against nine poisons. A worm came crawling, it killed nothing. For Woden took nine glory-twigs, he smote the adder that it flew apart into nine parts'*
> - *Excerpt from the nine herbs charm*

The nine herbs prayer was documented within the Lacnunga, translated as remedies. An ancient medical text that covered around two hundred treatments using plants. The Lacnunga wouldn't confirm the use of spells, charms or magick simply referring to them as cures.

Much of witchcraft and folk magick is steeped in animism, the belief that herbs and plants hold their own unique spirit along with the land, animals, rocks, bodies of water, mountains, caves and trees. Genius Loci is the name for spirits of place and these were often worshipped as gods, many Celtic and Germanic gods and goddesses presided over sacred places throughout folklore before the move to Christianity. Nature was pretty much the church of old.

Druids were known for nature being their temple, they would worship the trees themselves holding counsel within tree groves. Trees most sacred to them were oak, ash, elder, yew alder, hazel and apple.

I have found working on my connection to the land incredibly beneficial to my craft, not just through gardening but also familiarising myself with the land around where I live. You might wish to get to grips with the land native to where you live, perhaps even documenting it within your book of shadows and observe across the year any changes you observe.

I live a few minutes from the sea but if I travel ten minutes away from home I am in the depths of the countryside therefore I have been able to enjoy but also compare the contrast in these two different terrains. You can make contact with land spirits no matter where you live, most of my life was spent in the urban jungle of south London where there is a wealth of parks, graveyards and historical sites, even leylines so there was always plenty for me to have been able to explore.

You might wish to research events such as tragedies, wars, heroes or even lore relating to gods or goddesses that are linked to where you live. I believe that areas where tragedies or significant events have occurred must have a lot of energy that has seeped into the land itself. Be it good or bad energy, I believe it becomes imprinted on the location.

Ley lines are sacred ancient sites on a map that are joined together by straight lines that connect one magickal site to another. They were often marked by pagan temples or stone mounds and it is said that we can draw spiritual and physical benefits from the ley lines that connect each point along with the sacred site itself.

There are additional beliefs around ley lines, in the UK and Ireland it was believed that these were pathways across hills and bridges for the fae. People were warned not to get caught walking these paths at twilight hours or during the night lest the fae carry them away. Another belief was that these lines are the veins of the earth where its powerful sacred energy is offered up and available to us. You might be surprised to find there are ley lines close to where you live. They make a great place to hold ritual as you can draw upon their energetic power for divination using pendulums, high energetic charge on the ley lines can make for interesting readings. It's recommended to prepare for visiting a ley line the same as you would for ritual in order to be as spiritually clean as possible before you embark on your journey, but also so you can pick up on as much sacred energy as possible.

You might opt to leave offerings for land spirits you may come across in the form of flowers, eggs, fruits, vegetables, herbs, shells or other items from nature.

Green Witch

You might decide following some work with the land that you are indeed a green witch. The green witch tends to have a nature based practice and understands the connection to the earth, trees, plants, herbs, animals, insects, rocks even the fae/earth elementals.

I have a strong belief in animism and therefore believe the plants and herbs I grow have their own unique spirits and energetic patterns. My mum had worked previously as a professional gardener for a sheikh who had a mansion out in the sticks, she then went on to start up and run community garden projects in our local area utilising scraps of land throughout our town as growing areas for herbs and plants that the community can share between them but also provide produce to local food banks. I have been fortunate enough to learn a lot from my mum in relation to plants and gardening as a result.

The best piece of advice she has ever given me is to observe - if you can check in daily on your plants it really is the difference between having to be proactive and reactive. A lot can change quickly in nature but by checking daily you can ensure your plants aren't under attack from caterpillars, aphids, slugs or snails, keep an eye on their roots, any damage or scorch marks to leaves, over or underwatering and their light needs.

It's good to study as much as you can when you do bring on any new plants, understanding where they are native to will help you understand their requirements in relation to soil, feed, light needs and as a result where to plant. You can grow practically anywhere even if it's just a case of using a windowsill should you have no outdoor space.

Whenever I am out enjoying nature I look to see if I might be able to support the fae and mother earth in any way, perhaps through picking up litter or helping any animals or insects I see in need. I have a long running history and reputation with my friends and family for saving seagulls from injury and also coming to the rescue of bees with sugar water.

I make sure I spend as much time as I can outside all year round, I work from my laptop in the garden, read, tend my plants, relax, write and entertain outside. I also spend regular days out at places in nature, photographing and sometimes collecting items for spell work. You might opt to add to your altar flowers, fruits, herbs, plants, rocks, crystals and perhaps even feathers or animal bones you may have found to bring your love of the outdoors inside.

Make sure that if you take anything from the land you ask for permission in some form be it from the fae or the land itself.

> *'Everything that slows us down and forces*
> *patience, everything that sets us back into the slow*
> *circles of nature is a help. Gardening is an*
> *instrument of grace'*
> - *May Sarton*

Sea Witch

I spend a lot of time by the sea yet you can class yourself as a sea witch no matter where you reside. It's possible to use other bodies of water such as rivers, ponds, lakes or streams or simply meditate visualising the sea within your mind's eye and draw on its power. Witches often view the sea as holding abundance energy, so great to draw upon when it comes to spell work for money or love.

Familiarise yourself with the spirit body of water you visit and note any animals, insects, birds and mammals you come across. You might wish to document anything you come across within your book of shadows, sea witches sometimes refer to their book of shadows as a book of tides. You might find the sea offers up items such as bones, feathers, driftwood, shells, hag stones, or seaweed you can add to your altar.

Hag Stones are created by the sea and other elements pounding through a rocks centre leaving a hole. Traditionally they were used in folk magic for anything from protecting people, livestock and property, warding off spirits of the dead, banishing illness and for healing purposes, fertility magick, preventing bad dreams and night terrors. Sailors would use them for protection of self and ships and it was believed you could see into the realm of the fae through the hole in a hag stone.

Sea shells can make beautiful tealight holders or tiny offering or libation bowls, driftwood can be carved to create the perfect wand and seagull feathers can be incorporated into your smoke cleansing practices and used as a fan to direct the smoke. Make sure you offer up thanks to the sea for anything it provides you with, I believe the best way I can help nature is to clear up any rubbish I might see whilst I am out so urge that you try and help in a similar way to offer up gratitude.

I keep a jar of sea water on my altar from a magickal day I spent on a beach near to where I live with my daughter. I incorporate it into my spell work but also use it to anoint my altar tools for abundance. You might opt to bring your altar tools such as cauldrons, jars, candles and your wand along with you to the beach in order to anoint them individually under the sea's water. You might also wish to have a small jar of sand at your altar to use when drawing your magic circle.

I like to meditate and pull tarot cards on the beach near me. Meditating and listening to the waves coming in is truly heavenly. You might opt to carry some of your spellwork out whilst at the beach or by a body of water and draw upon the waters powerful energy. A small way you might want to start is by drawing sigils for that which you wish to invoke onto the sand itself, let the sun activate your desire and the tide set the spell in motion.

Once it gets to the month of May you can count on me getting into the sea, which isn't for the faint hearted considering the UK temperatures. The sea is perfect for washing off negative energy due to the huge amount of salt it contains, perfect for cleansing your aura and it makes me feel energised and alive regardless of the temperature.

There are a wealth of deities linked to the sea that you might wish to consider working with, there are also sea spirits such as kelpies, selkies, undines, water nymphs, merfolk, merrows and nix that you might want to look more into.

The element of water is heavily linked to our emotions so is good to use within spell work relating to emotions, grief or shadow work.

Sea water is good to incorporate into spell or ritual work around banishing, protection, cleansing and healing.

River water is great for spells and rituals relating to creating wards, moving on within your life, focusing energy and empowering altar tools.

> *'See these waters they'll pull you up,*
> *Oh, now if your bolder than the darkness'*
> *These Waters - Ben Howard*

Weather Witch

The weather witch draws upon the weather's energy channelling it into their ritual or spell work. It's less about asserting control over the weather itself, more about directing its energy into your specific intentions.

Shamans, druids and many ancient tribes called upon the weather to assist in their magick, any weather events before scientific knowledge were considered work of the deities and each pantheon has a plethora of gods and goddesses dedicated to the weather. If you do work with a weather deity you might opt to make offerings asking for them to protect you and your home from storms or severe weather or even for them to end or redirect weather when it arises from affecting you.

You might opt to try carrying out some spell work using the weather's energy. Spell casting during a lightning storm is said to empower spell work relating to protection, power, manifestation, cursing, grounding and strength.

Overall rain storms offer cleansing and a fresh start or clean slate - it's also linked to spell work pertaining to purification, love, compassion, friendship, beauty rituals and releasing guilt and jealousy.

There's nothing I like more than witch weather, oppressive gloomy grey clouds that roll in and you can feel the electricity in the air. I find listening to the sound of thunderstorms and the rain restorative and truly magickal. There's something wild, unpredictable and somewhat epic in those moments and I am highly attuned physically to when a storm is coming in. Living by the sea we often have sea fog that rolls in which is wonderfully spooky.

In lore it is said that witches of the Celtic times would summon fog to protect women and children in a bid to hide them from invading soldiers, also to hide and protect travelling heroes or royalty on their quests to reach new lands where they may have had an unfriendly welcome.

Fog is seen as liminal, we often see it used within films to signify when something magical or supernatural is about to occur. Fog is seen as a space where the veil is thin and a connection is present between this world and the otherworld. It is said to hold transformational power presenting the mundane as something more mysterious and confusing. It was believed to have links to the witching hour and when fog was present it was said witches were casting their spells.

Use fog for work linked to the thinning veil - communication with spirit, astral projection, divination using pendulums and tarot or oracle readings relating to past life work. Fog can also be used for cursing spells. You might opt to charm an object to ensure its hidden or protected by leaving it outside in the fog.

Witches were known to have sung fog removal songs that were accompanied by a little jig. They would incorporate their besom into the dance in a bid to redirect the fog elsewhere. They would also pray to weather deities to ask the fog to return back to the sky.

Fog at sea could cause tragedy easily, sea witches were often called upon to disperse fog ensuring the safe return of sailors and their ships.

Weather Water

Rain water can be used for rebirth and growth spells, abundance, money, luck, new ventures, blessings, aids in the grieving process, mourning, releasing suppressed emotions and spell work that requires you to gain power over a period of time.

Rain showers have healing properties, they can be used to carry out aura field cleansing and to release and cleanse your energetic field. Simply stand outside under a light shower, close your eyes and feel the rain wash off the negative energy you have been carrying around.

Storm water is powerful and perfect for spell and ritual work pertaining to confidence, emotional strength, manifesting, raising energy, self-esteem, charging, letting go, moving on, revenge, breaking bad habits, balancing energy, power, motivation, curses/hexes, and also strengthening a spells power.

Storm water can be created by charging water you have in a covered bottle or jar under the power of a thunder and lightning storm or heavy wind.

Snow can be used for spells and rituals that relate to purity, banishing, endings, peace, encouraging sleep, pleasant dreams, hopes, ideas, glamours, hiding/finding objects. Perfect for slow working spells.

Dew Water has been used throughout folk magick, healing and witchcraft. Perfect for delicate spell work relating to the Fae, fertility and love.

> *'Dew is considered pure, newly created matter. For the Celts, dew was a gift from the in-between world; it came neither from the earth, nor did it fall as rain from the clouds. The in-between world is a magical place where nothing is yet fixed, but everything is possible - it is the in-between space in which healing can also take place'*
> *- Wold D Storl 'The Untold History of Healing: Plant Lore and Medicinal Magic from the Stone Age to Present'*

In order to collect dew water you will need a bowl, white cloths (white is said to be the best colour to use when collecting dew as it brings good fortune).

You will need to collect dew water before full sunrise. Run your cloth along the grass, plants and trees in order to soak up the dew. Once your cloth is fully saturated with dew water, wring it out into your bowl. Continue to soak up as much dew as you need repeating the process until you have enough for your spell or ritual work.

Sun Magick

Sun magick is great to work on for spell work relating to courage, happiness, creativity, strength, protection and dispelling any darkness from your life. Although the sun holds a masculine energy there are many solar deities that can be worked with, especially within Celtic and Norse pantheons.

Litha is classed as the time to work on your biggest spell work that requires the most energetic input from you. This is when the sun is at its most powerful, following Litha the sun begins to wane as the wheel of the year turns towards the darker half of the year.

The sun, like the moon, has its own cycle, two cycles in fact, the wheel of the year and the day. It's more practical and convenient to work on sun magick using the day cycle where the sun increases in its power up until noon when it reaches the highest point in the sky.

It decreases in power as it wanes low towards the horizon. Sunset is considered a liminal time.

Magick carried out at sunrise is when both you and the sun's energy is fresh and new, this is the perfect time for spell work relating to work or education as both tend to require an early start. Also for spells relating to ridding yourself of negativity, addictive habits or behaviours. Use the sunrise to enchant items that are linked to ridding yourself of negative energies or habits.

Noon is when the sun reaches its energy peak - use this time for spell work relating to health and wellbeing.

Sunset is a liminal time and said to be when the veil between the two worlds is thin so carry out work related to communicating with spirits, ancestors and deities especially around guidance and inspiration but also for closing the gap on where you are in life currently and the life you wish to create.

You can create sun water the same as you might moon water, fill a jar with clean tap water and place a lid on it. Leave it under the sun's rays for a little while and use the same as you might moon water. You may opt to add this to your altar at Litha to represent the divine masculine energy of the sun god. Working with any sun deities you might want to add images of the sun, yellow or gold items, summer flowers especially sunflowers and marigolds, citrus fruits and crystals such as citrine or tigers eye.

I have also charged my altar tools and crystals under the light of the sun, leaving them out for just one or two hours just not under direct sunlight.

Sun Invocation Spell

This is a great spell for invoking the sun's power for creativity, personal growth and positivity. Carry this out on a Sunday, ideally on a sunny day upon your altar to honour the sun.

Tools
> An orange or yellow candle
> Sunflower oil
> Citrus scented oils
> Marigold petals

You might wish to carve into your candle the sun glyph and perhaps sigils that relate to that which you wish to invoke.

Combine the sunflower oil and citrus scented oils and petals in a bowl. Coat your candle in the oil using your hands and visualise that which you wish to invoke using the sun's power. visualise solar blessings as you burn this candle upon your altar.

Cauldron of Transformation

The cauldron always brings to mind the powerful Welsh enchantress Cerridwen, whose name derives from the word Cerru meaning cauldron. She is known under many guises such as the triple goddess, the wise crone, the white lady of inspiration and death, goddess of nature, goddess of renewal, dark moon goddess, grain goddess and patron goddess of witches amongst others.

A powerful underworld goddess who is the keeper of the cauldron of knowledge, inspiration and rebirth, a shapeshifting goddess who is able to take on many forms. Cerridwen is an underworld goddess with reign over the realms of fertility, death, regeneration, inspiration, magic, knowledge, enchantment, she is often associated with herbology, astrology, prophecy, science and the moon. Cerridwen represents maternal devotion, inspiration and the search for wisdom and knowledge.

Like the Morrigan she is a powerful shapeshifter who takes on many forms such as a hawk, greyhound, otter, hen and even the form of a white sow when she addressed her people. A sow is said to be symbolic of spiritual enrichment and fortune.

Due to the wisdom Cerridwen holds she is often awarded the crone status which equates her with the darker aspect of the triple goddess.

Cerridwen's tale really is more about her two children than of herself, she had a beautiful daughter named Crearwy (meaning light) and a malevolent and ugly son named Afagdu (meaning darkness). Cerridwen was compelled to give her son Afagdu a gift to make up for his appearance and she decided to begin work on a spell that would offer her son all knowing wisdom from the first three drops of the potion.

The spell would take a year to come into fruition, Cerridwen sought out assistance with keeping the cauldron that contained the contents of the spell constantly stirred by roping in a blind man named Morda. He had an apprentice named Gwion Bach, a young boy who would help with the potions creation.

Gwion Bach worked hard to keep the spell stirred within the cauldron, upon the day of the cauldron's contents being ready Gwion stirred the cauldron and three drops of the potion splashed out the cauldron onto his thumb. He reacted quickly without thinking by sucking the liquid from his thumb until it dawned on him he had taken in the spells power.

He panicked knowing Cerridwen would know what he had done and he decided to make haste and scarper. Holding all the power he held he knew he could shapeshift into any animal he needed to in a bid to escape. He transformed first into a hare and in response Cerridwen became a Greyhound and gained upon him. On reaching a river Gwion became a fish and Cerridwen an otter, she was about to swallow him in his entirety before he burst up through the water as a bird. Cerridwen transformed into a hawk and made chase until he couldn't keep up and dropped back down to earth ending up in a barn hiding out in exhaustion.

Cerridwen entered the barn and Gwion used the last of his power to transform into a grain of corn, Cerridwen metamorphosed into a hen and ate each grain of the corn eating him up whole. Despite this Gwion wasn't destroyed and Cerridwen became pregnant, knowing this was indeed Gwion she plotted to kill him upon his birth. When he was born he was so beautiful she couldn't find it within herself to take his life, she did however sew him into a bag of skin and threw him out into the ocean where he was later washed up and found by a prince. In his new form Gwion Bach went on to become the prophet and bard Taliesin.

Cerridwen's story is symbolic of the healing process and the life, death, rebirth journey but also how our darkest experiences can often transmute into such gold later on.

Cauldrons are often used as an altar piece, a tool within our spell work we can use for making up potions, burning incense and candles or even within kitchen witchery for making magical meals. Symbolically they represent rebirth, transformation, wisdom and are associated with the element of fire and water. They also hold association with darkness, night and the all encompassing sea. Modern ideas are that they are a feminine tool however within mythology we have the story of Dagda of the Tuatha De Denan within Irish mythology. Dagda is often depicted as a druid, king, and father figure. He holds associations with fertility, agriculture, masculinity, strength, wisdom and magick. He owned the cauldron of plenty (sometimes named the cauldron of abundance) which was fitting for this Irish god who had a good appetite. Anyone who took from this cauldron is said to have left satisfied be it for food, health or wealth. Dian Cecht, another Celtic god, possessed the cauldron of healing.

The cauldron in more recent times has been seen as a symbol of the divine feminine, it is linked to Circe, Baba Yaga, Medea and of course Cerridwen. Cauldrons were often found across the Celtic isles in both well shafts and rivers having been left for the goddess.

Cerridwen's story overall is said to present the turning of the seasons and nature's yearly cycle of death and rebirth. Her children Crearwy and Afagdu are said to represent the light and dark in the universe.

Cerridwen is said to make herself known to you if there is the need for you to change, that you need to allow something to die in order for the new to be born. She is great to work with should you need to examine your life to determine what no longer serves you, her energy is linked to sowing the seeds of change and pursuing their growth with your personal power. She is also good to call upon for assistance within your spell work overall due to her motherly nature.

The shapeshifting scene with Cerridwen and Gwion Bach might bring back memories of the Disney film, the Sword and the Stone where we see Mad Madam Mim chase Arthur with them both in different animal forms. Many mythological scholars argue that the tale of Cerridwen has the influence of the legend of King Arthur and the search for the holy grail. Both the cauldron and the grail are associated with the water element and provide whomever uses them with powerful benefits.

Working with Cerridwen as a deity, she is said to bring inspiration, dreams, visions and the power of prophecy and divination. She is good to work with for matters relating to fertility, herb magick, creative writing, wisdom and knowledge.

Offerings you can make to her include poetry or creative writing (she birthed one of the most famous bards after all) corn, grains, acorns, feather and perhaps three drops of liquid representing the three Gwion Bach spilt bestowing him with magick, knowledge and wisdom.

Releasing Spell

Tools
> A Cauldron or heat proof bowl
> Paper and pen
> Matches or a lighter

This is a simple spell I regularly carry out upon a full moon, cast your circle or begin your ritual as you would normally. You might wish to take some time out to meditate on what you wish to remove from your life (perhaps bad habits, financial issues, toxic relation-ships). Be certain you are ready to remove this from your life, make sure you have clarity on it and once you are ready write down on your paper in black ink what you wish to release.

Once you have written out all that you wish to release you may wish to say the following incantation or create your own bespoke releasing spell -

> *'Under this night and the full moons light*
> *I remove and release all that I write*
> *From this night on I step forward with new goals*
> *in mind*
> *With the love, support and guidance from the*
> *divine*
> *So mote it be'*

You might wish to chant this incantation a few times in a bid to raise the energy within your circle. Once you are ready, set alight to your pieces of paper indi-vidually over your cauldron or heat proof bowl and watch them burn down to embers. Rid yourself the next day of the ashes somewhere away from your home.

Cerridwens Wishing Spell

As we remove from our life it's also good to call in the new, the universe abhors a vacuum. You might opt to work this spell upon a new moon to call in all that you desire or following the releasing spell.

Tools
A cauldron or heat proof bowl
Corresponding herbs or plants linked to your wishes
(check out the Magick chapter for an outline of six basic herbs that you can use for practically any spell you might carry out). you might have an association you create yourself, for example you might decide to use rose petals when it comes to a spell pertaining to romance, lavender when it comes to peace within a friendship or relationship or basil when it comes to money.
Matches or a lighter
Paper

Cast your circle or begin your ritual how you would normally, I recommend beginning your spellwork through meditating again but this time begin by visualising two pairs of shoes in front of you. On the left hand side are your old shoes that represent your old self, to your right are your new shoes that represent your new life including your new wishes, it could be a beautiful box fresh pair of trainers or a pair of witchy lace up boots. You decide!

See yourself putting these new shoes on, to begin we want to visualise our first desire through visualising living in that first wish you want to put out to the universe. See yourself in those new shoes walking that path you long for, perhaps your wish relates to how you want to live your life, or a material wish you desire to bring in. How does life look now that you have this wish? What are the colours you can see? how does it feel to own this particular object? How do you act in this new experience?

See your wish in as much depth as possible, in this visualisation you already have your wish. How happy does it make you feel? allow the feeling to absorb into every part of your being. How does your life look now that your wish has come to life?

Within your meditation visualise each wish coming into fruition, run through each wish you want to bring into your reality. Once you have worked through each of your desires, finish up your meditation and start writing out on each slip of paper your individual wishes.

Once this is complete, set your individual wishes on fire and burn them within your heat proof cauldron adding the herbs or flowers to the mix. By adding the herbs and/or flowers we are in essence creating a potion similar to that of Cerridwen's and our cauldron transforms these ingredients along with our wishes in the same way. You might wish to carry out this meditation for the next month just before you go to sleep visualising your wishes coming to fruition.

Wishing Grain Spell

Tools
Grains - Oats, Seeds or Wheat
Cauldron or a bowl

Place your grains into your cauldron or bowl at first light and speak over the grain what you wish for. The grain within our spell is of course symbolic of Gwion Bach transforming into the small grain that Cerridwen gobbles up.

Place the cauldron or bowl upon your altar and whisper your wishes upon it at regular intervals throughout a full day. Upon the next morning cast the grain to the wind for the birds to eat and deliver your wish to Cerridwen the goddess.

Fear Removing Cauldron Spell

You will need -
An item or image that represents your fear
A cauldron or bowl
Salt or sand *(enough to submerge the image or item you are using within this spell)*

Sit with your cauldron or bowl in front of you positioned so you can comfortably gaze into it. We want to focus on the bowl or cauldron to visualise that which we fear and wish to banish.

Consider how your life could look once you have con-
quered this fear.

- What could you do differently without this
  fear?
- How will you feel?
- How will your life be different?
- What are the opportunities open to you once
  this fear has been slain?

Hold in your hand the image or item you have chosen
to visualise your fear.

With intention channel all the negativity you associate
with this fear into the item or image you hold, really
exhaust all of those feelings and focus on transferring
them into the item or image.

Once you feel this part of the process is complete, lay
the item or image into your cauldron or bowl and pour
salt or sand over the image or item until it can no
longer be seen.

Speak the following incantation or craft your own
words that feel most relevant to you -

> *'The fear of .... has held me back too long*
> *with these words I bid this fear gone*
> *I lay this fear to rest buried with no hold*
> *I step forward from this day in strength and bold*
> *So mote it be'*

Suffocate this fear by ensuring your item or image is
fully covered in the salt or sand. Allow it to die out

leaving your mind and your future and observe it stripped of its power and diminished.

If you are able to safely bury the contents of this spell following your magick work this can solidify this spell even further.

Cauldron Divination

Scrying using a cauldron is a particularly ancient form of divination. Scrying is the act of gazing into either a crystal, smoke, a candle, a fire, a black mirror or a reflective surface such as water to seek out guidance or messages.

We can carry this out as a form of clairvoyance using our mind's eye to seek out symbols, shapes, colours or we can draw upon clairaudient skills as we may find our mind offers up verbal messages.

With cauldron divination you can opt to use fire or water. For water scrying simply add water to your cauldron, settle your mind and cast your gaze upon the water as though you were staring into a mirror. Blur your focus and continuously stare into and through the water within the cauldron seeking out any images that may appear either within the water, or within your mind. Keep your mind open for any messages as they come in any form.

You might like to note anything that comes up within these sessions within your book of shadows and practice scrying, honing your skills as you go along and of course your intuition.

You might opt to fire scry within your cauldron and gaze into the smoke or flames, consider the direction or strength of the flames, any colours or shapes you might see. I have tried fire scrying through burning herbs within my cauldron.

Another method is to fill your cauldron with water, burn a candle and drip its hot wax onto the waters to surface to divine. Seek out any shapes or letters that might form.

Medicine Woman

Our everyday rituals really make up the heart and foundation of our craft. The bigger rituals and spell work we carry out can provide different markers to our healing process but the daily spiritual practice we carry out builds our spiritual muscle and provides us with medicine for both soul and mind.

It's like starting a healthy eating journey, your mind and soul improve as you go along with your daily spiritual practice, just as your body would through eating healthy foods consistently. Within this chapter I want to outline some of the specific medicine for the soul you might wish to administer to yourself daily, weekly and monthly. These are the different routines and small changes I made for myself that weave throughout my craft and mental health care.

Dream Analysis

'A dream which is not interpreted is like a letter
which is not read'
-The Talmud

During long bouts of sobriety I returned to having
vivid dreams, something I hadn't experienced much
since being pregnant with my daughter and up to my
mid teenage years before I discovered drugs and alcohol. As a child and late teen I had many messages
through dreams and I often knew events would occur
before they did following seeing them unfold in a
dream usually the night prior. I have always been very
connected to my subconscious through them.

Once I stopped abusing alcohol my dreams became
amplified with messages and angel numbers delivered
to me through seeing a number in my dream either on
a clock, as an amount of money, written on a cheque
or receipt, various different ways with the most
unusual being on a jackpot machine. These numbers
would stay in my mind all day. These dreams only ever
occurred in my lifetime once I had started fully
embracing getting sober, connecting with my deities
and following my path with the podcast and work
relating to my craft.

The angel numbers in my dreams usually ran into
three or four digit numbers, not easy to remember yet
from the moment I woke up to the end of the day this
number was imprinted on my mind. The minute I
woke I knew to search that particular angel number
up online to establish what its message was. I didn't

understand at first what these numbers meant, I only discovered angel numbers were a thing when I put a status up on social media laughing about my dream the previous night, in my dream my favourite singer Ben Howard handed me a cheque for a certain amount of money and I was wondering what it was all about! I was just puzzled until an acquaintance of mine messaged me after seeing my status to suggest I look into the angel number that was written on the cheque and see if the number and its message might be relevant to anything I was going through. As a witch, angels and angel numbers had never really come up on my radar.

To this day I still have dreams that contain numbers and I use my book of shadows to document the numbers that come up and track numbers that have come up for me previously. I use the internet to research what each angel number means and take on board what they are trying to impart.

Dream analysis alongside divination is such a powerful tool, especially when you are carrying out the shadow work process as it can uncover messages from your subconscious that are deep rooted and hidden.

> *'Dreams are illustrations…..from the book your soul is writing about you'*
> *-Marsha Norman*

Dream Interpretation Guide

- Keep your book of shadows or dream journal and a pen to hand by your bed

- On waking write out all you can remember, you might be surprised once you get started how much starts to come up

- Document any symbols, emotions, people that arise within the dream

- Consider how you feel on waking after the dream – happy, scared, confused etc. The feeling you have within the dream is equally as important as how it is interpreted

- Before you search up dream meanings ask yourself what you think the dream was trying to tell you? What situation do you think this is linked to within your waking life? What is the purpose of this dream? What is it trying to tell you?

- Who was in your dream and how did you feel towards them within the dream? Does this represent underlying feelings you might have in real life? Every individual we see within a dream usually represents a part of ourselves

- Use a dream dictionary or google your dreams for further insight, ultimately reflect first on how you felt within the dream and all that resounds with you at a soul level for your analysis.

- Keep documenting your dreams regularly, you might identify symbols, people and emotions that repeat themselves. Consider using your book of shadows or dream journal as a dream dictionary as you build up the information on symbols and emotions.

'The interpretation of dreams is the royal road to a knowledge of the unconscious activities of the mind'
-Sigmund Freud

Recurring dreams tend to arise when you are stuck with an issue in life, it's your mind's way of finding a solution and if you work on understanding your recurring dreams you can begin to discover your core beliefs and mindset and work on implementing positive changes to improve your life.

Nightmares arise when your mind needs to offload stress and fear, analysing your nightmares can help us to observe our mindset and provide insight into how we can heal issues, conflicts and overcome fear and stress. Fear is often a sign of us being alive and something we need to walk towards, embrace and listen to what it is trying to show us.

Smoke Cleansing

Before I enter any meditation process I like to smoke cleanse my body and around my altar using smoke cleansing bundles, if you work with sage bundles it's worth noting sage is like a spiritual bleach so when working with it I make sure to follow up with another smoke cleansing method that brings in a positive energy – you might wish to try lavender for soothing, calming relaxing tones, rosemary for opening the heart and feeling expansive or lemon balm for uplifted emotions and feeling light and bright. Harvest your herbs in the summer months, perhaps at Litha when they hold the most magical power and tie round them with colourful twine, leave to dry for a couple of weeks and use to smoke cleanse when needed. Alternatively burn herbs along with charcoal disks within your cauldron or a heat proof bowl.

Meditation

Meditation is at the core of my sacred morning rituals, it can especially help to eliminate the fight or flight response that contributes to anxiety and helps create a sense of calm. Meditation is a period of time to ourselves where we can connect to our true being and higher power, it can help us to come up with solutions but also connect us with our desires. It's one of the strongest tools to release repressed emotions and provide clarity, peace and also to support creativity. Some of my best work has come from divine inspiration offered up in meditation.

I like to light a tealight and an incense stick within my daily morning meditation practice. My mind now associates the scent of incense with the time to be still and enter into meditation or ritual.

I tend to not use guided meditations as I like to allow for still silence, if I do use sound I like to listen quietly to shamanic drumming. If you struggle or feel resistance to begin your personal meditation practice I recommend breaking it down and trying it out for two minutes per day, building up to five minutes, then ten and so on. A good form of meditation that got me started is the Anapana meditation method where you solely focus upon your breath.

Meditation allows us time with our highest most authentic self, through doing this we can start to hear our soul talk with us. When we meet anyone new we are so eager to hear their hopes, dreams, goals, fears, passions yet often don't allow our soul to discuss these with us.

Daily Devotion

I take time following my meditation to speak with my deities, I discuss with them my day, what's come up for me in my emotions, what's coming up that I am looking forward to or worried about, what's troubling me. I might ask for guidance on actions I need to take, I compliment them on their qualities and from time to time ask if they might help me that day or if I can invoke the energy of one of their particular positive epithets to help me with a task or challenge I am facing.

Divination

I carry out a daily tarot pull following on from my meditation and daily devotion. Simply shuffling the cards, pulling one and researching its meaning and listening to how my soul interprets the card and its relevance. This is one of the best ways to learn to read tarot and was recommended to me by my brother Allen who has taught tarot through workshops.

Some of the best wisdom I have heard in relation to tarot is firstly from an Estonian witch who recommended you pull cards with your left hand as it's the side closest to your heart.

The hands of a witch hold much power, our left hand is said to be used to bind, banish, diminish, remove and curse and our right to summon, conjure, bless and encourage. Our thumb is connected to earth and physicality, our index finger is connected to air and communication, intellect, thought and the mind, our middle finger is connected to spirit and their magick, guidance and clairvoyance, our ring finger is linked to water so our inner self, emotions and intuition and our little finger is said to be linked to the element of fire, passion, love and strength.

You might find it beneficial to sit and communicate with your cards beyond asking them what they want to tell you. Almost shuffling them as you talk to them about all you have been up to, just holding a conversation with these magical tools about how your day was, what your current intentions are, how you're feeling and asking their opinion on things as you go along. Keep shuffling and pouring all that energy into the cards as you talk with them, we like to see our cards as magical tools yet we often just shove them into a box and pull them out whenever we deem appropriate so as we begin to grow they can too with us. If we stop talking to them they will stop too. It's good to talk to them and witness over time your relationship grow.

In relation to the tarot and oracle cards please do buy your own cards, It's an absolute myth that you must have them gifted to you and this likely originates from times when tarot cards wouldn't have been as easily accessible to buy and often handed down. My first deck was gifted to me yet I have bought many oracle and tarot card decks myself since. I like to smoke cleanse any magickal tools before I introduce them to my altar or magick work. With tarot cards and crystals I like to leave them under my pillow for the first three days of having them and spend time shuffling them and interacting with them, it has taken me a good six months to build connection with a new decadent tarot deck that I bought last year, I am at a point now where the cards are spiritually connected to me. You can also bond with your cards through studying the images, lots of cleansing and shuffling and even keeping them on your person as you go about your life for a little while so they get to 'see' and join you in your life and your energy.

I recommend keeping your tarot cards covered when not in use and you may want to consider boundaries you have around them, are you dragging them along to parties or around toxic environments and people where they might pick up on this energy which might feed into your readings?. My good friend Erin, an amazing tarot reader, went so far as to recommend out of respect having a separate deck you use purely to work with a deity or an ancestor and to treat your decks like a trusted spiritual advisor, with the utmost respect and only come to them in sincerity. She also recommends cleansing your tarot deck through putting them all into chronological order and upright paying particular attention following that should any cards come out in reverse.

Tarot cards are such a fantastic tool to assist us with shadow work, self help therapy, decisions, comparisons, choices, divination before or after a spell or ritual, exploring our emotions and communing with our ancestors, spirit guides or deities. Overall I believe they are key within our practice to assist us in honing our intuitive skills. They can be as logical or mystical as you choose to make them and rest assured that you do have an element of free will to change the outcome of the cards.

I prefer to ask my cards open ended questions as opposed to yes/no ones as these provide us more insight into what actions to take. Also because each card holds a light and shadow side.

Tarot cards really are our subconscious showing us the way alongside our dreams, divination and dream analysis can be such a strong tool to identify that which your subconscious wants you to know. If you are carrying out shadow work tarot can be a great tool within your arsenal that you can use to focus on answers and indications of the roots of the inner child work you might want to focus on.

Glad List

My favourite take on the gratitude list, the G within glad stands for gratitude so I start by listing in my journal in the present tense all that I am grateful for. The L stands for learning so I note all I have gained knowledge of throughout the course of my day, A stands for achievement so you can note all that you might have achieved and D stands for desire. I like to write my desires within the present tense outlining all that I dream of as though I am already in possession of it, be it a material possession or even some form of skill or outcome.

This has contributed strongly towards my successful manifestation processes but also highlights and makes me appreciative for what I have learnt and achieved each day, which in turn helps to bolster my self esteem and confidence.

Grounding

Grounding is a good way to support your physical, mental and emotional wellbeing and to balance and equalise your energy. Grounding is a very necessary part of my mental health practices as my energy can leave me high as a kite and unable to come back down to earth or seriously depleted, I have to work regularly on finding the middle ground.

If you are ungrounded it can show up as you being erratic, scattered, unfocused, moody, distracted, on edge and disconnected. Grounding will help you feel settled and focused in mind and body. In periods of stress and anxiety we can find ourselves in our fight and flight mode all too often, grounding can counteract this and calm our mind and body.

Grounding can also support our magick work, if carried out before any spell or ritual work it can help us to focus and reduce any internal distractions. It connects us to our higher self and intentions for the work we are set to carry out. You might also opt to carry out grounding following your spell work, sometimes our energy following spell or ritual work can be too high or draining so grounding again can return us to a calm state and bring us back to reality.

As a witch, grounding using nature is one of my favourite practices, here are some different ways we can connect with the earth to support grounding –

Earth

Walking barefoot on the earth, this is something I like to do during spring, summer and autumn months. I wander around my garden barefoot, I often take my shoes off when I visit the beach even up to the beginning of winter. Earthing is a physical experience of just putting our bare feet or naked skin against the earth. Electrical fields mess with our natural field of energy, everything has an electrical field and earthing basically recharges our body.

It's said that forty five minutes to two hours a day is the period of time you can really benefit from having your bare feet connected to the ground but here in the northern hemisphere with a cold climate this is sometimes tricky, I feel any period of time grounding can be beneficial.

Air

If you find yourself rattled, panicked or can sense you are shallow breathing try taking deep breaths in for four counts and proceed to breath out for twelve. This process was taught to me by my counsellor when I was on the verge of a panic attack. It brings me to a calm mindful state quickly and opens up my lungs in order to remove stale air replacing it with fresh and new supply.

Meditating using the Anapana method where you solely focus on your breath is a powerful way of grounding with the air element. This form of meditation involves focusing on in and out breathing. Buddha is said to have advised monks to carry out this form of meditation by sitting in the forest by a tree and watching if their breath was long or short. If you decide to carry out the same method within the woods you can ultimately tap into grounding through combining the elements of air and earth.

Fire

Fire really resounds with me within my practice and is my favourite element to work with, I put this down to having all fire signs in my astrological birth chart. Leo star sign, Aries moon sign and Sagittarius rising.

As an element, fire represents change, destruction, power, strong will, renewal, passion, anger, transformation, rebirth and sex and its linked to the planet Mars.

A wonderful method of working on grounding and an ancient form of divination is fire scrying. One of the most ancient and easiest forms of scrying, flames have a hypnotic effect which explains why we are often mesmerised at the sight of a fire or flame.

All you need to get started is a candle flame, bonfire or hearth fire. In ancient India they discovered that the pineal gland feeds on light following practices of staring into a flame for long periods of time. This can stimulate our third eye and through regular practice of gazing at a flame we can increase our alertness, psychic abilities, intuition, creativity and even improve our sleep.

In order to begin fire scrying you might want to sit and hold a question or intention in your mind, focus on how bright and intense the flames are and see which images you can pick up within the fire, If you decide to ask any questions within your scrying session it is said that bright upward shooting flames signifies a yes response, darker dull flames accompanied by lots of smoke signify a no response.

You might see clear images within the flame or find the flames conjure up images within your mind's eye that you can interpret. You may even hear sounds such as singing or talking and fire scrying can also just cause certain ideas or thoughts to come into our head, perhaps messages we receive from our subconscious or even the otherworld that might not make sense to us in the moment. It's worth journaling following on from your fire scrying experience within your book of shadows or journal and allow a few days for your unconscious mind to process what came up.

If you find you cannot connect to any messages that come up from your session consider if this is a message meant to be passed onto someone else you know if it feels of relevance. Like any form of connection with the otherworld we might at times become the vessel to channel the message.

When you are ready to finish up your fire scrying session give yourself time to look away from the fire to adjust your eyes, common sensations following fire scrying can be a sense of high energy and clarity. Be sure to carefully extinguish the flames or let them die down safely.

Another method of grounding I often use is to sit or read by candlelight, I find this incredibly grounding, it keeps me in the present as I can only see my immediate environment illuminated by the candlelight but also provides me with a form of ancestral or past life connection as I feel that space and time leaves within that moment and I return to perhaps a life I have once lived or align with how my ancestors darkness would have been lit.

Water

My walks to the beach involve sitting on the pebbles with my dog and watching the waves roll in and out, taking in the sounds of them lapping against the shore and the seagulls squawking. I am sure even Bowie benefits from this practice!

Sitting by a body of water scientifically makes us feel good anyway as it emits negative ions that are beneficial to our bodies as they help us to release cortisol, reduce inflammation and increase blood flow.

Submerging yourself into water is another wonderful way to connect with the element of water. Wild swimming or simply floating within a large expanse of water such as the sea, river or lake is a wonderful way to ground using water. I swim in the sea locally where I live, if I am honest only through the summer months. At the same time just having a bath is a fantastic simple way to ground using the water element!

You Are The Medicine

'Cure yourself with the light of the sun
and the rays of the moon.
With the sound of the river and the waterfall.
With the swaying of the sea and
the fluttering of the birds.
Heal yourself with the mint and mint leaves, with
neem and eucalyptus.
Sweeten yourself with lavender,
rosemary and chamomile.
Hug yourself with the cocoa bean
and a touch of cinnamon.
Put love in tea instead of sugar and
take it looking at the stars
Heal yourself, with the kisses that the wind gives you
and the hugs of the rain.
Get strong with bare feet on the ground and with
everything that is born from it.
Get smarter everyday by listening to your intuition,
looking at the world with the eye of your forehead
Jump, dance, sing so that you live happier
Heal yourself with beautiful love.
and always remember….. you are the medicine

Maria Sabina
Mexican Curandera and Poet

Soul Loss

Through my healing process it always felt like part of my healing was always out of reach. I couldn't understand why I felt as though a part of me had been taken away following certain events within my life. It's fairly common for people to claim after a traumatic event, seperation, death, accident that they lost a part of themselves that they cannot retrieve or that they feel incomplete.

I discovered soul loss through a conversation with one of my dearest witchy friends, Rachael, a hedge witch and shamanic practitioner. I retold the story to Rachael of my ex partner who I struggled to get over, how in our final conversation he told me we would never be over and we would one day reunite. I felt this vice like grip with his energy in the aftermath of our relationship and I wanted out, it hung over me to the point that I couldn't bring myself to date or if I did I was plagued by thoughts of him. Even though the new people I met were much better for me, I struggled to hold any feelings or thoughts for anyone else. He haunted my dreams and I used to feel as though I had something tied around my ankle which sounds absolutely crazy. To the point I used to physically brush off my ankle to check nothing was there, it felt like being tethered and in my mind I could see a shackle around my ankle. Ironically we had both had matching tattoos on the opposite ankle done together which occurred to me on writing this.

The energy around our seperation never felt normal to me, it didn't compare to other breakups I had had. I was desperate to cut the cord. In my frustration I discussed this with Rachael with no expectation for her to have any answers. It was however Rachael that made me realise words hold such power which of course as witches we know, him cursing me saying we would never be over in essence was like a curse being cast over my life and future but also him holding some sort of psychological power over me and my soul. This is when Rachael explained to me all about soul loss and soul theft.

Soul theft can be the result of a separation, death of a loved one, relationships with poor boundaries, abuse or codependency. We can also, without realising it, hang onto a soul part of the other person, other times it may be as a ploy to remain connected to them despite our separation.

On the day of writing the last chapter of this book I had an intense vivid dream where I met with my ex partner, we were standing together against some railings and I turned to him smiling declaring 'oh, here I am with the man who broke my heart' to which he responded by laughing and saying 'you broke my heart first'. I then became angry and I let rip within the dream, telling him exactly how he had broken my heart to which he responded by explaining how much easier his life was since we were no longer together and that he was happy with his new wife.

I cried and ran off and then decided shortly after to try and find him again. I felt numb and despondent when I tracked him down and knew it was futile explaining again to him how he had hurt me. In the dream he simply asked me if I wanted any drugs, which of course is something I always associate him with. I didn't respond but watched as he dug into his top coat pocket to retrieve said drugs, he then lent over and blew across my head and face. This made me feel in the dream as though I had been knocked out or was under the influence of drugs.

This dream was so strange, a lot changed for me thereafter. I began to feel indifferent about our relationship, less stuck with my ex's heavy energy. I filled my shamanic friend Rachael in on my dream to which she commented 'Carly, it's almost as though he has agreed to give you your pieces back, It's literally like a soul retrieval' I appreciate this wasn't a soul retrieval carried out by a shaman but it did give me some peace thereafter.

Soul loss can occur following physical, mental, emotional or sexual abuse, death of a loved one, addiction (alcohol, gambling, drugs, eating), an out of body or near death experience, being over disciplined in childhood, rejection, abandonment, acting against your morals or entering a relationship with issues around personal boundaries.

Soul loss is said to be a form of spiritual illness that fragments the soul, this affects you physically, psychologically and emotionally. Following trauma it is believed by shamans that your vital essence separates from you, these fragmented soul parts exist outside of linear time within a non-ordinary reality. Our mind does this in a bid to protect us as it feels it cannot handle the level of trauma and pain it is experiencing.

Shamans believe that soul loss cannot be effectively treated through counselling or psychotherapy as the soul parts are fragmented and exist within the other realm, meaning they cannot effectively be brought into the treatment and subsequently remain separate from our being.

Signs of soul loss include chronic depression, fatigue, apathy, feeling empty, disconnected or incomplete, dissociation or memory gaps, loss of meaning or purpose within life, emotionally suffering, PTSD, nightmares or flashbacks from trauma, suicidal tendencies, destructive behaviours, addictions, unhealthy connection to a former partner or family member, inability to end a relationship, immune deficiency problems, dissatisfaction with life, things that previously gave you joy or that you had an interest in no longer mean anything to you, inability to feel or express love or emotions, cynicism, prolonged grief, little in life that lights you up/inspires or impresses you, feeling abandoned or unprotected by the divine/deities/universe or ancestors dependent on your beliefs or who you may work with. Many will use alcohol, drugs, compulsive sex, overeating and various vices to mask the pain and to fill the empty space where our soul parts are missing.

Soul retrieval is an ancient shamanic practice where the shaman enters the non-ordinary reality where our fragmented soul parts are said to reside following on from trauma. Through a shared meditation and visualisation the shaman can guide us through realms that are heavily guarded and inaccessible, they will walk with spirit guides and journey in a bid to seek out missing soul parts for an individual that need to to be returned, this often involves the shaman meeting the individual at different ages within their lifetime, at the age when the soul part was fractured and lost. Along the way they will come across guardians of the soul who might appear to them visually as beasts, reptiles or monsters - they show up in these forms but ultimately are defence mechanisms of the psyche. They may also come across gatekeepers who guide and show them the way.

The shaman may enter the lower world, the realm that is the realm of the soul where all our history is stored. This is said to be the realm where ancestors and spirit animals reside. They often enter this realm through a body of water and this realm is linked to collective consciousness.

The middle world is akin to the earth plain, shamans often use this realm to heal ailments or seek out solutions as to what's causing an individual suffering.

The upper world is linked to destiny and our individual spirit, similar to heaven as a realm and it holds angels, spirit guides and cosmic beings. Here we can find spiritual divine guidance in a less practical realm to the lower world.

When it comes to soul theft the shaman will meet with both parties involved, the theft also affects both involved parties. Soul retrieval when it comes to soul theft is a trickier ritual where a shaman may need to reason with the soul thief asking them to see sense and return the stolen soul parts or perhaps assisting the soul thief with their own healing so they can give up the stolen soul parts.

Trickery is another method the shaman may use should the thief not offer up the soul part voluntarily. This can be through asking their spirit animal to distract the thief as they steal the soul part back, the shaman will still remain conscious and compassionate to the soul thief's welfare in the aftermath as much as they can.

The shaman will work on reintegrating the soul parts back into the individual they are working with through either ritual, chanting and/or breathing the soul parts back into the individual by blowing across the heart and crown of their head and visualising the missing parts returning and becoming whole with the soul. Once the individual has their soul part returned they are strongly encouraged to relinquish any habits or addictions they might have created as a result of the soul loss and the shaman will work with the individual to create new behaviours that are more healthy. They clearly do not need their former toxic behaviours as the reason for carrying them out has been removed. Soul retrievals are said to be able to bring back soul parts lost within this lifetime but also from our past lives. This means we can incarnate parts of our soul from a particular lifetime or even abilities that we might not have been able to incarnate with as we lost them many lifetimes ago.

The shaman may outline to the person they performed the ritual for exactly what they saw on their journey to retrieve their soul parts. They will often have witnessed visually what happened to that individual for their soul part to leave them.

Preparation for a soul retrieval is said to be vital to ensure going forward your newly integrated lost soul parts can merge together more successfully. It also assists the shaman with being able to seek out and return parts quicker and easier. By preparing it is said that your soul parts will also be more keen to return to you and ready to come back.

Recommended ways to prepare for a soul retrieval include grounding, shadow work, journaling, working on releasing, letting go and forgiveness, working on creative projects that may help you release trapped emotions, recording your dreams (especially as they are our direct link to our subconscious), meditating, shamanic journeying (in a bid to enter altered states of consciousness which will occur during your shamanic soul retrieval).

Praying to your ancestors, spirit guides, deities or whomever you hold divine connection with, singing, dancing, laughing, and consciously crying all help to transmute trapped or blocked energy through your body which is great for healing. Reiki and past life work can also help you before you embark on your soul retrieval experience.

Taking good care of your mind, body and spirit, so eating good food, ensuring you have a good healthy sleep pattern, spending time in nature, laying off alcohol, drugs or junk food and being conscious of who you spend time with. You may find you come to a soul retrieval experience following handing over your power to someone within your life, ensure you analyse your relationships regularly to identify times where you might hand over power to others either consciously or unconsciously - patterns often occur within our relationships if we aren't learning the lesson. You can begin to understand how your own insecurities and wounds allow this to happen and come up with solutions on how to avoid this in the future. Soul retrieval or even focusing on soul healing offers up so many benefits to us as individuals but also for the collective consciousness. Shamans recommend carrying on with similar practices to those used before your soul retrieval to help seal in and integrate the returned soul parts. They would also implement dancing, singing, chanting, banging a drum or using a rattle at the end of the soul retrieval process to seal in the returned soul parts.

Shamans have existed throughout every inhabited land across the globe for around 100,000 years, the word Shaman originates from the Tungus tribe in Siberia. I have come across various meanings of the word shaman from 'one who sees in the dark', 'he or she who knows' 'one who sees beyond the veil' through to simply 'healer'. The hedge witch comes to mind for me as the shaman when it comes to my own practice, we all have indigenous ancestors and my own ancestry is steeped with Irish and Scottish blood so I look to what healers within these native lands would have done in times past, the link to these shamans is of course very broken.

Throughout history hedge witches would have lived on the outskirts of a town when villages were separated by forests, where a forest began was referred to as a hedge and symbolically the hedge is also seen as the boundary between this world and the spiritual realm. The term hedge witch originates from the saxon word haegtessa which translates to hedge rider. They would have been seen as healers with a connection to the veil, charmers, herbalists that held the ability to astral travel, craft nature based magick and would be frequented for any physical ailments through to soul loss or even removing a spirit from your home. The hedge witch would mainly work with the earth element, throughout European witchcraft they were referred to as cunning folk or wise women who honoured the herbal arts that were medicinal and spiritual in nature. You would visit the hedge witch for their assistance as a midwife, for any physical ailments where the belief was that all illness would arise from soul troubles. The wise woman would work on removing the shadows to alleviate the illness using conjurations, blessing and prayers but also animism utilising the power of rocks, trees, incense, spring water and holy water. You would also frequent the hedge witch for anything of a supernatural nature or to have your fortune told. In ancient times within tribes, shamans were often counted on to divine and reveal where food resources could be found.

The hedge witch would often practice as a solitary witch and their nature based practice would often have been passed down to them from their own ancestors and further honed. Hedge witches are said to have a remedy for anything under the sun with much of it being prepared under the light of the moon. They would generally have collected all they needed from the hedgerows around them. I am keen to champion utilising the herbs and plants within your own native lands as the hedge witch would to create that connection.

Hedge witches had a real connection to the land and would have worked with deva's, plant spirits that would have helped the hedge witch with healing magick. Hedge witches would often grow their own herbs and healing plants and they would have considered each plant's individual correspondences and medicinal properties. When it came to harvesting the herbs and plants they would use within their practice they would collect these at first dawn often barefoot, many wise folk would not wash, pray or greet anyone whilst seeking out the plant they needed for their work. Upon finding what they needed they would speak to and explain to the spirit of the plant what they required it for, who the remedy would be used by and they would utter related incantations whilst harvesting it.

Many wise women professed to be guided in their dreams to various herbs and plants for remedies they required. Some also proclaimed to have seen spirits of the otherworld in broad daylight whilst out in nature who would advise them on what plant or herb they should use for what ailment. Reports of this nature were particularly rife throughout the plague of the middle ages.

Wise women were said to be active throughout most villages in Ireland and Irish Folk Stories reference how the bean feasa (wisewoman) and bean leighis (woman healer) could carry out soul retrievals through trance states where they visited the otherworld.

The bean feasa were traditionally healers that worked with the land, sidhe (fae) and the otherworld. They would often be unmarried older women who were highly regarded and relied on for their healing abilities and knowledge of plants and herbs to use as medicine but also for their imbas (divine inspiration).

In 1902 Wood -Martin described in his writings the herbs these wise women would have growing in their gardens;

'tansy, solomons seal, belladonna, hearts-ease, dandelion for liver complaints, comfrey as a styptic, samphire boiled in milk for heartburn…. mountain sage for palpitations or for coughs, bog bark or parsley boiled in milk for gravel, nettles with ginger for wind in the stomach, horehound as an expectorant, mullein as a caught mixture……. A bunch of fairy flax lies on the top of the salt-box; sown into the wise woman's scapular is a four leaved shamrock, an invaluable specific for rendering fairies visible to the human eye'

The hedge witch was known to have powers as a seer and many came to have these abilities following some form of serious illness, trance or trauma.

Journeying

Whenever we go to sleep our soul leaves our body and frequents other realms as a form of journeying, our soul will also leave our body as a form of protection should we experience intense trauma. Soul retrievals tend to be carried out by an experienced shaman however we can embark on our own form of shamanic journeys to help us gain wisdom, guidance and healing.

Journeying is a powerful tool I have used for close to ten years now, it was something I stumbled upon whilst at a spirituality festival. I happened to end up in a small igloo type tent where a shaman went through a journey to introduce us to our spirit animal and I wound up meeting my tiger who is with me to this day along with a large beautiful chuckling african woman Mama Roots who used to give me huge hugs and unconditional love which clearly I so needed at that time in my life.

Journeying has been so transformational for me, at its core it offers up wisdom, guidance and reassurance. I have found myself being able to self soothe emotionally, tap into my intuition, find comfort with my spiritual team, uncover symbolic signs and find solutions or inspired action I can take in relation to intentions I have set. I have come to journeying within some of my darkest hours, beginning the journeying process with no hope and thoughts of despair and finishing up with tears streaming down my face, a light heart and feeling loved, protected and with fire in my belly to transition my life forward.

There are guided journeys that you can listen to that will help you get started, you might wish to have a go at one that might help you discover your guides but the map below for your journey will likely help you with uncovering who your spiritual team are regardless.

A guide can come to you in many different forms - as an animal, deity, mythical creature, ancestor, elemental or angel. Some guides will have been with us since we were children and others come into our life at different points of our life depending on what we need. My tiger has remained with me since I met him over ten years ago. Mama Roots was only with me for a short space of time when I needed some real love. In more recent months I met with an interesting goddess who was always on the periphery of my journeys. I could sense she was there within the caves of the lands I journeyed to but for a while I was nervous to meet her. She's a chaotic goddess who laughs a lot and shapeshifts into pink puffs of smoke when she gets over excited, she scries over a cauldron of pink oily liquid within a cave surrounded with tropical flowers and she inspires me with my self worth, confidence and creativity.

You can call upon your guides at any point, I have always pulled my tiger into consciousness if I am out in my day to day life and need to feel confident or remove fear. I can often visualise and feel him walking alongside me when I need to and it instantly shifts my energy and makes me feel safe and ridiculously courageous. Imagine having a real tiger walking alongside you and fighting your corner and tell me that wouldn't create an energy shift!

Journeying is entering an altered state of consciousness, when you first come to journeying it's worth mentioning that you may not meet first time round with your spirit guide, you might not view your journey akin to watching a movie but you should draw upon all the other senses open to you such as seeing, hearing, feeling, touching, tasting and smell. The shaman believes that all seeing within journeys is done via the heart. Pay attention to any symbols that may arise within your journey, try to ignore the left side of your brain that may be bringing your mind back to rationality. In the beginning I often felt doubts arise as I set off on my journey that I was making everything up that I saw, as I went along I managed to appease my overactive brain simply by agreeing with it, blocking out that nagging rationale and venturing forward regardless. The rewards from journeying cancelled out any doubts or rationale my brain wanted to throw into the mix. Our mind often tries to limit our ability for freedom. It's worth noting shamans are often viewed as liminal beings who can exist between both worlds, many believe the inner world to be true reality. They never doubt what their mind shows them so rest assured you're doing just fine with anything that comes up within your own mind whilst on your journey.

Patience is key when it comes to journeying, again your first attempts may feel fruitless however practice makes perfect and each attempt works on opening up your senses for the spirit world.

Map for Journeying

- Set an intention for your journey, remember this is not about fortune telling. It's looking at an area of your life that perhaps you want to seek out guidance, wisdom or healing for. You may wish to write down in your book of shadows what your intention is, we never want to give our guides the full reins on what we are doing within our life. We need to come to them in a self empowering manner whereby we are not asking them for a yes or no answer, more an open question as to what guidance they can provide for us to consider or even asking them for a sign. You may have two paths open to you within your life so perhaps ask them to give insight into what you should consider for each to help you weigh up your decision.

- Ensure you are in a prepared sacred space for your journey. Perhaps light candles, incense or burn herbs. I like to ensure my altar is in order, I smoke cleanse myself and around my sacred space and enter into a meditative state before I get started. I listen to shamanic drumming playlists as I find the drumming takes me elsewhere and makes the transition much easier.

- Speak a blessing before you get started asking for your spirit guide, ancestors, angels, deities or whoever you work with to look after you once you begin your journey and thank them for their assistance and protection.

- You might wish to lie down or sit up for your journey. I tend to lie down and ensure the room is very dark with a little candlelight.

- There are different realms that shamans will travel to whilst journeying - the three world map which involves travelling to the upper, middle and lower realms or the celtic map which involves entering the underworld where you sail across a lake on a boat called Immrama. You may wish to seek out more information or follow a guided meditation in relation to these realms, I simply started off journeying through visualising somewhere I actually would like to be, my go to place is in the depths of the jungle upon a stone platform that has caves set within the walls. As I have continued journeying the landscape has built up and become more vivid. I have visited other lands too, finding myself standing in front of and entering a huge golden temple, also in a forest with a beautiful lake running throughout. You can't go wrong with where you go on your journey so let your imagination go wild.

- Should you meet anyone upon your journey you might feel curious as to whether they are your spirit guide, you should see what intuitively comes up for you in their presence but you can also ask them directly if they are your spirit guide, feel free to ask them four times for complete clarity, remember you can have more than one guide but also different guides might show up for you at different times within your lifetime dependent on what you are experiencing. Come back to journeying as many times as you need to until you feel you have found your guide, there is no right or wrong way of doing it.

- When you feel you have seen all you needed to see, asked and received all the information or guidance you can I would recommend retracing your steps that you first took within your journey. Once you are ready, open your eyes and write down everything that came up for you within your journey. Take care to write down any symbols you might have received, write on who your guide showed up as, what senses did you employ? were there any synchronicities?

  You might wish to look into any symbolism that came up the same as you would with dream analysis or how you intuitively feel they should be interpreted.

- Once you have finished your journey you may wish to thank your spirit guide, ancestors, angels, deities or whoever you work with for protecting you whilst on your journey.

- Once you have finished, do something to bring you back into your body and this reality, take a bath or shower, go for a walk and eat a nutritional meal.

———— ◆◇◆ ————

I used the process of journeying to help gain guidance for how to heal and find closure in respect of the relationship with my ex partner. During my journey I found myself within a university, everything I saw was pink and this felt connected to my heart chakra and love. I witnessed myself studying and I intuitively felt that I was being shown I needed to focus on my research work as a podcaster and author, the work that ultimately brought me many opportunities, happiness and a feeling of self accomplishment. This certainly wasn't the answer I was expecting when I set my intentions before embarking on my journey, however I did heed the message. Once I threw myself into my work I always felt happier and less plagued by my ex partners energy.

Later on I carried out a shamanic journey to meet with my ex, have one final conversation that could offer up closure and cut the cord between us. In the other realm we stood across from one another within a corn field, he seemed angry at me and intuitively I knew this was due to his own insecurities, he was often insecure, jealous and resentful of me in our relationship within the real world. I could also pick up that he didn't want the cord to be cut in order for me to remain an available option to him following his shotgun wedding. This was an intensely moving experience where I got to tell him exactly how he had made me feel, allowing him to say anything he needed to also. I told him I was letting him go and just wanted to move on but that he needed to let us go too. I cried so much in this and the other realm but I felt such a relief at being able to say what I had never had the opportunity to.

Journeying has proven extremely beneficial to me, from finding solutions relating to my work, purpose, relationships, friendships, finances and any issues that might have arisen within my life. Guidance has come through in ways that I have never envisaged and given me a starting point to take action.

The Witches Pyramid

The soul loss part of my healing journey really began to feel like the final chapter for the bulk of my healing process, where the ground had begun to clear and I could see space to begin to plant some new seeds for the future.

This is when I stumbled across the witches pyramid after reading an old witchcraft book called 'Mastering Witchcraft' by Paul Hudson.

We touched on manifesting within The Moon chapter when we looked at setting out your intentions under the new moon, the witches pyramid could be perfect for working towards much larger magickal intentions you might have.

I recommend working on bringing in the new once you have worked through a lot of your shadow work and healing process, once your energetic vibration is raised higher as a result. The universe abhors a vacuum and will always look to bring in the new, therefore it's good to make sure the new is exactly what you have planned to call in and not random!

Once you have worked through a lot of healing you will likely have better clarity on what you wish to bring into your life. If your healing process is anything like mine, the person I am now following my healing process is worlds apart from who I was when I started out, things I wish for now couldn't be more different!

The witches pyramid has four cornerstones - a virulent imagination, a will of fire, rock hard faith and a flair for secrecy.

Imagination

Imagination is a true gift to us all, consider those daydreams an absolute blessing. You might start out working at the witches pyramid with no inkling of what you would like to bring into your life, change or manifest and that's a great place to start from. I came from this place and would begin with meditating within my sacred space in front of my altar in a bid to ground and connect to my higher self. Once I felt calm and ready I would start to visualise two pairs of shoes in front of me, my current pair of white converse trainers and next to them on the right a pair of brand new box fresh trainers that I coveted.

I visualised myself stepping into those beautiful new trainers and began to visualise who am I when I have those trainers on. What my ideal day looked like, what I look like, what am I doing for work? what does my bank account look like? how is my home looking? who am I with?

But the most important question - how do I feel? Everything we do as witches is connected to energy. By concentrating on how I wanted to feel I started to actually experience that feeling and I felt hungry for it. Playing on the fact that our mind cannot separate what we visualise from our reality I began to tap into that and experience those feelings without yet having the end result. I got to the point within those meditations where I felt a natural high, all that raised positive energy was coursing through me and it absolutely got me fired up to take inspired action.

To build on my manifesting practice I interchanged scripting with visualising depending on how I felt. I found I could raise the same form of vibration and desire through both methods. As an avid writer I felt the words on the page held much power and I could get specific on the finite details of exactly how my life was going to look.

Scripting prompts you may wish to consider before you start crafting your dream day scripting process could be as follows -

- What does my dream day look like?

- What does my dream career look like?

- What are the words I want to live by?

- What is one goal I would like to achieve and how would I feel if I achieved it?

- What is one habit I would like to start?

- How do I need to change to live that dream life?

- If anything was possible what would your life be like?

These questions should throw up clarity to help us conjure up images that make us excited for what we can bring into existence. If the word witch means to bend or to shape we truly, as witches have the power to bring that into our existence. Once you hold this clarity through questioning what you truly want you can then regularly engage in scripting, writing in the present tense using words such as 'I am', 'I have'. Words are power for any of our magick work and using vocabulary such as 'want' or 'need' when it comes to working the witches pyramid leave us per-petually wanting or needing. Write as though everything you wish for is happening right now in this very moment.

Enchant yourself by creating secret visions of how you and your life can become, the higher the energy and excitement all the more potent your dreams will be coming into fruition. You are the sorcerer of your life and the possibilities are endless.

You might build on this practice by creating yourself a dream board or box where you keep items or photos that link to what you wish to manifest. I have had goal boards that I have kept upon my altar, especially as I tie a lot of my spell work into what I am trying to bring in, it also means I look at it everyday to remind myself and submerge that into my focus.

Once you start getting full clarity on what it is you want you might have spell or ritual work you want to tie into your manifesting process. So what habits do you need to get rid of that won't be serving you towards your manifestation? What blocks do you have relating to self worth, procrastination, perfectionism, addictions, habits that are holding you back from the path you have decided you want to tread? Maybe use the full moon to work on removing these from your life to help push you forward. Perhaps using new moons to put out to the universe what you wish to bring in along with perhaps new skills you wish to acquire or develop to help you get to where you want to be. You can carry out spell or ritual work according to your manifestation and maybe work with the moon or even magic days of the week or spell times.

Will

The will of fire relates to your emotional investment into what you wish to manifest. So emotional investment combined with your intense focus equals your will of fire.

This part of the process involves some deep inner reflective work and honesty. You must believe that what you wish to bring in is viable, if you're scripting or visualising and it feels icky or the energy feels off come back to the beginning and reconsider. If the energy and conviction you have regarding this manifestation isn't right it's not likely to come into fruition but it could also be a potential disappointment and lead you to doubt your magickal abilities.

In order to hone our magickal will we must have full clarity on what we want, hone and focus our attention on that one thing because where attention goes energy flows. We must consider how we can take inspired action towards our desires but also allow the universe to meet us halfway. Don't get too hung up on the how's at any point because I truly believe if we proceed to go forth and take inspired action to obtain it, it's as good as ours. As part of your reflection, focus on what behaviours you might need to change or who you need to become to achieve this manifestation, work on gradually transforming and implementing behaviours of the version of you that is living this manifestation. This part of the triangle is ultimately about determination and mindset.

When I engage in any form of scripting I always finish up with 'so mote it be' at the end of the pages to signify this will take place. It might not come in exactly how I imagined it but in my honest experience when it comes to manifesting I often find what I have asked for comes in even bigger and better than I could ever have hoped for.

Faith

*'Through Faith the imagination is invigorated
and completed for it really happens that every
doubt mars its perfection'*
- Parcelsus

Most magical power solidly depends on faith, think on when you perform any ritual or spell work. Your faith holds together your work as we believe our magick will come to life.

In 'Mastering Witchcraft' Paul Hudson explains how 'imagination and will are intimately connected to faith, faith quietens any objections and acts as a catalyst to action, and temporarily and instantaneously helps as a prop to support you believe in the inevitability of your success. Without faith you wouldn't even embark on the path towards that which you desire as you wouldn't believe it could be obtained'

Writing on the cornerstone of faith for the witches pyramid, Paul Hudson stresses how as a witch it's important to never break your word. A witches word is never given lightly, therefore if you plan on implementing the witches pyramid within your practice you must ensure that any intentions you set you will stick to this path until the successful manifestation of what you wish to achieve.

The emphasis is on tapping into and cultivating a mindset where anything you say will come true, for every time you break your word, be it through your own fault or others, you chip away at the faith you hold within yourself which can be difficult to cultivate. The more you keep your word and create, the more powerful you will become.

Through setting and achieving goals new neural pathways are formed within your brain as a result of new thoughts and feelings. You can create new habits and beliefs that can help to rewire your brain and through continuing to work on these new behaviours accepting them as the new norm. If we fail to keep our mind focused on these new habits and behaviours as part of working towards our goals, often our strongest pre-existing and undesirable patterns and habits that are more familiar to us that affect our brain, body and behaviour will resurface and can sabotage what we are trying to create.

If our brain had a choice it would opt for the path of less resistance that's the most familiar to us, this is why we can find ourselves on autopilot when we go unchecked.

Regularly reviewing where we are within the witches pyramid process can be integral to keeping ourselves on track with our inspired actions and behaviours. It's worth checking in with yourself weekly, monthly and quarterly (depending on how long your manifestation is taking) to see how you are progressing.

At the end of each month I consider what I learnt within that period, any blocks, fears or distractions I experienced, how I made myself feel good, what I didn't achieve and why, people I learnt from and who inspired me, what actions I could start to take to improve, what insights I gained throughout the month. After reflection I focus on setting three goals or actions that might support my bigger goal and help break the process down once again making it more manageable.

I come back to planning usually on a Sunday night or Monday morning to outline my weekly to-do list that ties into those goals and also to prioritise what actions I need to take.

Secrecy

The key part of the process and the fourth cornerstone of the pyramid is secrecy, not to let on what you are trying to conjure up, outside energy can throw off your goals. Witchcraft consists of knowledge, knowledge is power and ultimately power shared can result in power lost.

This is not to say you cannot tell anyone of your plans but be aware of who you do mention them to. By keeping your magick work and desires to yourself you can save yourself from being influenced by others opinions but also ensures our dreams or goals remain true to us as we alone have constructed them with no exterior influence.

By remaining silent on your plans this also puts the emphasis on you being able to better pick up on messages from the divine, your higher self or indirect teachings from a mentor. By keeping our magickal workings to ourselves we are also solidifying this as a union or act between us and the universe.

Exactly how you work the processes of the witches pyramid is entirely up to you, I have interchanged and adapted the process yet the principles remain the same. Be sure to honour and mark the occasion when one of your manifestations comes into fruition and offer up thanks to the universe, spirit guides, ancestors, deities, yourself or whomever you believe has assisted you in securing your dreams.

Powers of the Sphinx

'You are familiar with the Four Powers of the Sphinx, attributed by the adepts of old time to their four elements.

Air is to know, Scire; Fire is to Will, Velle;

Water is to Dare, Audere; and Earth is to keep Silence, Tacere.'

- Aleister Crowley, Magick without Tears

The Witches Pyramid stems from the works of Eliphas Levi, A French esotericist, poet, author and ceremonial magician who wrote books on kabbalah, magic, alchemical studies and occultism.

He created the five pagan virtues, better known as the Powers of the Sphinx, Alastair Crowley would later come to expand on Levi's work. Parcelsus, an alchemist and Swiss physician, came up with the magickal agents of will and imagination around three hundred years prior to Eliphas Levi's developed work.

Eliphas Levi used the sphinx to demonstrate the four elements and assigned four parts to its construction

Know - *The head of a man (air element)*
Will - *Rear of a bull (earth element)*
Dare - *Torso and front paws of a lion (fire element)*
Keep Silent - *Wings of an eagle (water element)*

His work outlined how the sphinx is perfectly balanced with all four elements; man holds all four elements within yet man must strive to attain balance.

Levi and Crowley both agreed that once a practitioner had achieved all four steps, a fifth would subsequently be attained which is gaining a greater understanding of the divine self and an understanding and mastery of the god within. I like to consider the witches pyramid as more of a rinse and repeat process that can be applied to different magick as you move through life, once you experience the process working for you through your own personal completion of a desire. This brings us back to faith, once you have set out and achieved a manifestation as a result of these processes you will increase your faith and positive mindset. This may mean you build on striving to work on bigger goals or simply manifest quicker as a result of better understanding and conviction.

'To attain the *sanctum regnum*, in other words, the knowledge and power of the Magi, there are four indispensable conditions - an intelligence illuminated by study, an intrepidity which nothing can check, a will which cannot be broken, and a prudence which nothing can corrupt and nothing intoxicate. TO KNOW, TO DARE, TO WILL, TO KEEP SILENCE - such are the four words of the Magus, inscribed upon the four symbolical forms of the sphinx'

-Eliphas Levi

Transcendental Magick

Do Mote it Be

Healing is never a linear process yet the divide between where I am today and where I started is vast, akin to living another life within the same lifetime.

The drama I wrote of within the early chapters seems a lifetime away from where I find myself today, working through my personal dark night of the soul and shadow work has been the alchemical task of this entire process with the rituals and spell work peppered throughout this book as the metaphorical glue that bonded the process together. The medicine I have outlined offers consistent nourishment and connection within life and spiritual practice. The evidence of these small rituals and magick success is clear in that should I ever miss a day I hastily return to them seeking out their comfort and benefits.

You will no doubt find yourself at different chapters within your life where you need to return to shadow work and utilising these spells and rituals again. I must stress that should you feel you have lost your way on the crooked path of recovery or healing, these small diversions are to be expected, embraced and need to be normalised. A relapse or losing our way can often lead us to believe that we are going backwards but in essence a breakdown in my experience will always lead to a breakthrough and can shoot us further forward in our journey then we could have expected or hoped for with a new found knowledge or realisation of who we are and what we are capable of.

> *'An arrow can be shot by pulling it backward. So, when life is dragging you back with difficulties, it means that it's going to launch you into something great, so just focus and keep aiming'*
> *-Unknown*

If I could offer up one golden nugget of information should you ever find yourself lost, stuck in a rut or not knowing how to move forward, I wholeheartedly stand by returning to or beginning a daily practice of meditation, daily devotion (be it to your deities, ancestors, guides or angels should you work with them) and morning pages. Watch and wait for the path to become clear again, I cannot stress enough how this always brings me back to my higher self.

I fell off my path of recovery during the writing of this book, it was a brief period yet my intuition quickly knew to bring me back to these practices in a bid to draw upon my connection to the divine and reestablish connection with myself. Quickly I found myself in alignment and new plans and opportunities began to arise with no real forced input from me aside from these consistent small daily actions. In terms of relapse, in any form of healing we will never have failed unless we stop trying and we certainly won't be brought back to the same starting point we were at when we began our healing journey as we have already gained so much knowledge along the way.

One of the main blocks I find and see with healing is resistance, we avoid shadow work in fear it will consume us, a false belief I myself bought into. Be sure to consider any feelings of resistance to any of the prompts within this book as indicators of the areas where you should get to work for the best results. I had to deeply contemplate what I believed would culminate if I worked through the process. The fear I held was that I wouldn't be able to cope with the feelings that surfaced, that fear was cunning, baffling and powerful. I felt it held the capacity to push me to the brink, yet the surprise and gift when I faced up to its task was how much weight lifted off my shoulders and my chest, my mind and body almost let out an audible collective sigh of relief. The weeks following my shadow work were exhausting, confusing, with a haze of strange dreams whilst my subconscious processed events combined with elation throughout my waking hours that the shadow work hadn't been able to eat me alive.

My experience of healing larger forms of trauma has taught me to allow my emotions to wash over me and give myself ample time for them to be processed whilst minimising my need for external forms of anaesthetising. My ability to self soothe and rely upon my own internal compass and abilities to cope has to be the biggest strength working on healing has gifted me.

Should new scenarios create new trauma, revert back to the original practices within the shadow work chapter, document exactly what has happened and all the feelings you have around it and old beliefs that are being triggered for you. Exhaust every single feeling and emotion through getting it out onto the page, write on it as often as you need until you feel it washes over you. You may feel called to construct letters to those that have hurt you, perhaps those you might have hurt. Don't feel you need to send them, you might opt instead to burn them under a full moon when you feel you have exhausted this return to the shadow work process.

When I find myself seeking external validation, looking outside for the love that perhaps I am not giving to myself, a common behaviour following trauma but also a consequence of low self esteem and confidence. I opt to ramp up self care in the form of walks, time in daylight and nature, baths, space for solitude balanced out with time with people in my life that can support me energetically and emotionally, naps, water and good nutrition. I read when I was in early recovery (I feel the same applies overall for any intense form of emotional healing work) that you should treat yourself like a newborn baby, after all you are in the throes of creating a new life for yourself.

Tie this in with a return to the inner child work and reparent yourself, feed yourself how you would little you, give yourself lots of naps and so on. When we are going through a period of change our brain is in essence laying down new neural pathways which can exhaust both the body and mind.

Reflection is a wonderful way to observe and appreciate how far you have come. You may wish to do this through rereading your journal or the book of shadows you have worked through alongside this book to appreciate how far you have come. This mirrors the situation I find myself in whilst writing this chapter, rereading through this book I found it hard to believe The Worst Witch chapter was about me and my life because the person I am now couldn't be further from Carly back then. Reflection is such a powerful reminder of all the dragons we have slain.

Writing this last chapter has been a highly emotional process, in some respects it feels like a conclusion and ending of a chapter of my life that has tied in with my recent decisions and ability to stop allowing old loves to continue to still haunt me, to an extent I had at one point become a ghost in my own life watching them carry on living whilst I was still raking over the coals.

'Do you know it's possible for a person to become a ghost whilst they're still alive?'
-   Tom Hardy as Ron Kray to Frances - Legend

My life today is much calmer with less need for anaesthetising. I still live in a Victorian flat, the sea at the end of my road with my daughter Amelie, my french bulldog Bowie and my cat Tarot. I still work on the podcast and I write. I have in the course of writing this book had the opportunity to write for a magazine, it's as though the universe can sense the ending of one situation as with me finishing up this book another new exciting opportunity within the witchcraft world has just blown in on the wind that I am excited to commence. On the inside my heart and mind feels lighter, I have clarity on how I can manage my mind when things do arise and I possess the ability to self soothe and get myself back on track with ease.

My reason for writing the warts and all stories on where I have been, all that I have done and where I am now has purely been to provide testament that transformation can be made. I have witnessed many witches come through deeper, darker, more intense trauma than I have ever experienced, applying their craft in similar ways and ultimately going on to live happier fulfilling lives. Some wounds still remain and likely always will, but not their power.

My love, I conclude that for you to be reading this book you class yourself as a witch. In my mind this means you already possess great power to bend, change or shape your reality once you put your intention into it. In the words of Glinda the good witch from The Wizard of Oz

'You had the power all along, my dear'.

Resources

My Favourite Witchy Books

Hedge Witch - Rae Beth

Women who run with the Wolves - Clarissa Pinkola- Estes

Danielle Dulsky - Season of Moon and Flames

Entering Hekates Garden - Cyndi Brannen

Lunar Living - Kirsty Gallagher

Sacred Self Care - Chloe Isadora

Intuitive Witchcraft - Astrea Taylor

Wicca - Scott Cunningham

Folk Witchcraft - Roger J Horne

A Secret History of Witches - Louisa Morgan (Fiction)

The Witch of Salt and Storm - Kendall Kulper (Fiction)

We are the Luckiest - Laura McKeown (Sobriety)

Quit like a Woman - Holly Whittaker (Sobriety)

My Favourite Witchy Podcasts

Keeping her Keys - Cyndi Brannen
Dreaming the Ancestors - Tara Wild
Shaman Talk - Rhona McCrimmon
The White Witch Podcast - find me here, had to be done!
Home Podcast - a key tool within my sobriety (Non witchy but wonderful)

Music that Accompanied the Writing of this Book

Ben Howard - *Promise*
Ben Howard - *End of the Affair*
Ben Howard - *Esmerelda*
Ben Howard - *Time is Dancing*
Chelsea Wolfe - *Mer*
Chelsea Wolfe - *To the forest, towards the sea*
Deadboy - *Rye Angel*
Deadboy - *White Moon Garden* (My little brothers own music and the theme to my podcast)
Al Wootton - *Over*
Blind Willie Johnson - *Dark was the night, cold was the ground*
Bon Iver - *Roslyn*
Mozart - *Requiem K626: Lacrimosa*

Erik Satie - *Gnossiene: No 1*

Alexandre Desplat - *Fox in the Fields*

Peter Gundry - *The White Witch*

Danheim - *Ulfhednar*

Kerli - *Tuleloits*

Eivor - *Trollabundin*

Shannon Pearl - *The Parting Glass* (my beautiful friend)

About the Author

Carly Rose hosts The White Witch Podcast, it was nominated for Outstanding New Podcast of the Year 2020 with the podcast coming second at the 2020 Witchies Awards. The podcast has reached number one in the spirituality charts in the UK and other countries since its launch Samhain 2019.

An avid podcast listener, Carly was keen to start a UK witchcraft podcast that provided fellow witches with as much information in regards to the craft as possible with her mission to break down and make the craft understandable and give listeners confidence and encouragement to create their own practice.

Carly also runs The White Witch Coven on Patreon, a witchcraft community with extra podcast episodes and grimoire pages.

www.thewhitewitchcompany.co.uk

INSTAGRAM @thewhitewitchcompany
FACEBOOK - The White Witch Company
PATREON https://Patreon.com/thewhitewitchcoven

CPSIA information can be obtained
at www.ICGtesting.com
Printed in the USA
LVHW052015261021
701492LV00002B/3